W9-AFD-395

Shifts and periodicity for right invertible operators

D Przeworska-Rolewicz

Institute of Mathematics / Polish Academy of Sciences

Shifts and periodicity for right invertible operators

Pitman Advanced Publishing Program

BOSTON · LONDON · MELBOURNE

PITMAN PUBLISHING LIMITED
39 Parker Street, London WC2B 5PB

PITMAN PUBLISHING INC.
1020 Plain Street, Marshfield, Massachusetts

Associated Companies
Pitman Publishing Pty Ltd., Melbourne
Pitman Publishing New Zealand Ltd., Wellington
Copp Clark Pitman, Toronto

© D. Przeworska-Rolewicz, 1980

Library of Congress Cataloging in Publication Data

Przeworska-Rolewicz, Danuta.
Shifts and periodicity for right invertible operators.

(Research notes in mathematics ; 43)
Bibliography: p.
1. Operator theory. I. Title. II. Series.

QA329.P79 515.7′24 80-467
ISBN 0 273 08478 X

All rights reserved. No part of this publication may be reproduced, stored in a retrieval system, or transmitted in any form or by any means, electronic, mechanical, photocopying, recording and/or otherwise without the prior written permission of the publishers. The paperback edition of this book may not be lent, resold, hired out or otherwise disposed of by way of trade in any form of binding or cover other than that in which it is published, without the prior consent of the publishers.

Preface

Poisson [1] was the first mathematician who has observed the essential connexion between shifts, derivation and periodicity. Instead of the classic derivation operator we shall consider a more general class of linear operators, namely right invertible operators. We shall try to follow the theme of Poisson's ideas for these operators. We shall define shifts for right invertible operators acting in linear spaces (in general, without any topological assumptions) in two different ways, not equivalent in the general case. We shall indicate also some applications of the notions introduced, in particular, to functional-differential equations. We point out that all conditions of solvability are reduced to a problem of the invertibility of some polynomial in a right inverse, i.e. in applications, to a problem of the invertibility of some integral operator.

Contents

*Chapters 11 and 12 were written during the Canadian Mathematical Society Summer Seminar On Ordinary Differential Equations held at the University of Toronto, July 20 - August 12 1979 and in the Mathematics Research Center, University of Wisconsin-Madison, August 15-20 1979.

0 Preliminaries

The purpose of this section is to show some algebraic approaches to Calculus and to Differential Equations which permits consideration in a unified way of ordinary differential equations, difference equations and some partial differential equations and functional-differential equations.

We shall give here only the most important facts without proofs and also some examples. The bibliography will help the reader find extensions of this theory in several directions. A complete presentation of this theory is given in the author's book: "Introduction to Algebraic Analysis and its Applications" (in Polish, [12]).

Suppose that X is a linear space over an algebraically closed field $\mathscr{F}$. For instance, $\mathscr{F} = \mathbb{C}$. In the case where $\mathscr{F} = \mathbb{R}$, we can consider instead of X its natural extension to a linear space over $\mathbb{C}$. Denote by L(X) the set of all linear (i.e. additive and homogeneous) operators A defined on a linear subset $\mathscr{D}_A$ of X, called the domain of A, and a mapping $\mathscr{D}_A$ into X. Write: $L_0(X) = \{A \in L(X) : \mathscr{D}_A = X\}$. Denote by Z_A the kernel of A, i.e. $Z_A = \ker A = \{x \in \mathscr{D}_A : Ax = 0\}$.

<u>Definition 0.1</u>. An operator $D \in L(X)$ is said to be *right invertible* if there exists an operator $R \in L_0(X)$ such that $RX \subset \mathscr{D}_D$ and $DR = I$, where I denotes the identity operator.

The operator R is called a *right inverse* of D. The set of all right invertible operators belonging to $L(X)$ will be denoted by $R(X)$. The set of all right inverses of an operator $D \in R(X)$ will be denoted by $\mathscr{R}_D$.

<u>Definition 0.2</u>. An operator $F \in L(X)$ is said to be an *initial operator* for an operator $D \in R(X)$ corresponding to a right inverse R of D if $F^2 = F$, $FX = Z_D$ and $FR = 0$.

Note that the set Z_D plays the role of the *space of constants* for the operator $D \in R(X)$. Indeed, by definition, $z \in Z_D$ if and only if $Dz = 0$.

<u>Theorem 0.1</u>. Let $D \in R(X)$ and $R \in \mathscr{R}_D$. Then $F \in L(X)$ is an initial operator for D corresponding to R if and only if the following identity holds

$$F = I - RD \text{ on } \mathscr{D}_D .$$

This immediately implies

<u>Corollary 0.1</u>. Let $\{R_\gamma\}_{\gamma\in\Gamma} = \mathscr{R}_D$, where $D \in R(X)$. Then the family $\mathscr{R}_D$ induces in a unique way a family of initial operators $\mathscr{F}_D = \{F_\gamma\}_{\gamma\in\Gamma}$ defined by means of the equality

$$F_\gamma = I - R_\gamma D \quad \text{on } \mathscr{D}_D \quad (\gamma \in \Gamma) \tag{0.1}$$

The following theorem plays a fundamental role in our further considerations:

<u>Theorem 0.2</u>. (Taylor-Gontcharov Formula). Let $D \in R(X)$ and

$\mathscr{R}_D = \{R_\gamma\}_{\gamma\in\Gamma}$. Let $\mathscr{F}_D = \{F_\gamma\}_{\gamma\in\Gamma}$ be the family of initial operators induced by $\mathscr{R}_D$. Let $\{\gamma_n\} \subset \Gamma$ be an arbitrary sequence. Then for all positive integers N the following identity holds on $\mathscr{D}_{D^N}$:

$$I = F_{\gamma_o} + \sum_{k=1}^{N-1} R_{\gamma_o} \dots R_{\gamma_{k-1}} F_{\gamma_k} D^k + R_{\gamma_o} \dots R_{\gamma_{N-1}} D^N \qquad (0.2)$$

Putting $R_{\gamma_n} = R$ and $F_{\gamma_n} = F$ $(n = 1,2,\dots)$ we obtain

Corollary 0.2. (Taylor Formula). Let F be an initial operator for an operator $D \in R(X)$ corresponding to a right inverse R of D. Then

$$I = \sum_{k=0}^{N-1} R^k F D^k + R^N D^N \quad \text{on } \mathscr{D}_{D^N} \quad (N = 1,2,\dots) \qquad (0.3)$$

Theorem 0.3. Suppose we are given an operator $D \in R(X)$ and an operator $F \in L(X)$ such that $F^2 = F$ and $FX = Z_D$. Then F is an initial operator for D corresponding to the right inverse $R = \hat{R} - F\hat{R}$, where R is uniquely determined independently of the choice of $\hat{R} \in \mathscr{R}_D$.

Note that two commutative right inverses (initial operators) are identical. Thus our theory is, in essence, *non-commutative*.

Theorem 0.4. Suppose that $D \in R(X)$. Then

$$\mathscr{R}_D = \{R + FA : A \in L_0(X)\}, \quad \mathscr{F}_D = \{F(I-AD) : A \in L_0(X)\},$$

where F is an arbitrary (but fixed) initial operator for D corresponding to a right inverse R of D.

Theorems 0.1, 0.2, 0.3, 0.4 show us that it is enough to know either one initial operator or one right inverse for an operator $D \in R(X)$ to determine all right inverses and all initial operators.

The following theorem permits the reduction of all problems with superpositions of right invertible operators to problems with one such operator.

Theorem 0.5. Suppose that $D_1, \ldots, D_m \in R(X)$ and that F_j is an initial operator for D_j corresponding to a right inverse R_j, $R_j \in \mathscr{R}_{D_j}$ $(j = 1, 2, \ldots, m)$. Suppose that the superposition $D = D_1 \ldots D_m$ is well-determined. Write:

$$R = R_m \ldots R_1 ,$$

$$F = F_m + R_m F_{m-1} D_m + R_m R_{m-1} F_{m-2} D_{m-1} D_m + \ldots + R_m \ldots R_2 F_1 D_2 \ldots D_m$$

Then $D \in R(X)$, $R \in \mathscr{R}_D$ and F is an initial operator for D corresponding to R.

Now we shall consider linear equations with right invertible operators. Write:

$$Q(D) = \sum_{k=0}^{N} Q_k D^k , \text{ where } D \in R(X), Q_o, \ldots, Q_{N-1} \in L(X), Q_N = I$$

The following problem will be called a *mixed boundary value problem* (MHVP) for the operator $Q(D)$: to find all solutions of the equation

$$Q(D)x = y , \quad y \in X \tag{0.5}$$

satisfying the conditions

$$F_kD^kx = y_k\ ,\quad y_k \in Z_D\ ,\quad F_k \in \mathscr{F}_D \quad (k = 0,1,\dots,N-1) \tag{0.6}$$

In particular, if we put $F_o = \dots = F_{N-1} = F$, we obtain the conditions

$$FD^kx = y_k\ ,\quad y_k \in Z_D \quad (k = 0,1,\dots,N-1)\ , \tag{0.7}$$

and we call the problem (0.5)-(0.7) *initial value problem* (IVP) for the operator $Q(D)$.

A MBVP (0.5)-(0.6) (or: an IVP (0.5)-(0.7)) is *well-posed* if it has a unique solution for every $y \in X$, $y_o,\dots,y_{N-1} \in Z_D$. By definition, a well-posed homogeneous MBVP has only zero as a solution.

A consequence of Theorem 0.2 is

Theorem 0.6. Suppose that we are given $D \in R(X)$, $Q_o,\dots,Q_{N-1} \in L(X)$, $Q_N = I$, $R_o,\dots,R_{N-1} \in \mathscr{R}_D$. Let $F_o,\dots,F_{N-1}$ denote initial operators induced by $R_o,\dots,R_{N-1}$, respectively. If -1 is a regular value of the operator

$$\hat{Q} = \sum_{k=0}^{N-1} Q_kR_k\dots R_{N-1}$$

then MBVP (0.5)-(0.6) for the operator $Q(D) = \Sigma_{k=0}^{N} Q_kD^k$ is well-posed and its unique solution is

$$x = R_o\dots R_{N-1}(I + \hat{Q})^{-1}\hat{y} + y_o + \sum_{k=1}^{N-1} R_o\dots R_{k-1}y_k\ ,$$

where

$$\hat{y} = y - \sum_{m=0}^{N-2} Q_m[\sum_{k=m+1}^{N-1} R_m \ldots R_{k-1} y_k + y_m] - Q_{N-1}y_{N-1}.$$

Theorem 0.6 implies that the *general solution* of Equation (0.5) depends on N arbitrary constants, i.e. $\dim Z_{Q(D)} = N \dim Z_D$.

Corollary 0.3. Suppose that $D \in R(X)$, $R \in \mathscr{R}_D$ and that F is an initial operator for D corresponding to R. If -1 is a regular value of the operator $\hat{Q} = \Sigma_{m=0}^{N-1} Q_m R^{N-m}$, then IVP (0.5)-(0.7) for the operator Q(D) is well-posed and its unique solution is $x = R^N(I + \hat{Q})^{-1}\hat{y} + \Sigma_{k=0}^{N-1} R^k y_k$, where $\hat{y} = y - \Sigma_{m=0}^{N=2}[Q_m \Sigma_{k=m}^{N-1} R^{k-m} y_k] - Q_{N-1}y_{N-1}$.

Corollary 0.4. Suppose that $D \in R(X)$, $R \in \mathscr{R}_D$ and that F is an initial operator for D corresponding to R. Suppose, moreover, that the operator $I-\lambda R$ is invertible for every scalar λ and that $Q_k = q_k I$ for $k = 0,1,\ldots, N-1$, where $q_o,\ldots,q_{N-1}$ are scalars, $q_N = 1$. Then IVP (0.5)-(0.7) for the operator $Q(D) = \Sigma_{k=0}^{N-1} q_k D^k$ is well-posed and its unique solution is of the form

$$x = (I + \hat{Q})^{-1}(R^N y + \sum_{k=0}^{N-1} R^k y_k), \quad \text{where } \hat{Q} = \sum_{k=0}^{N-1} q_k R^{N-1}$$

(The operator $I + \hat{Q}$ is invertible by our assumptions).

Suppose that all assumptions of Corollary 0.4 are satisfied. Write: $Q(t,s) = \Sigma_{k=1}^{N} q_k t^k s^{N-k}$. Then $I + \hat{Q} = Q(I,R)$. We can obtain any solution of the equation $Q(D)x = y$, $y \in X$ by a decomposition of the rational function onto vulgar fractions. This decomposition gives us an "Operational Calculus" for right invertible operators (without any convolution and Laplace transforms).

If -1 is an eigenvalue of the operator $\hat{Q}$ defined in Theorem 0.6 then MBVP(0.5)-(0.7) is *ill-posed*. However, under an obvious necessary and sufficient condition, solutions of this problem do exist and we are able to find these solutions.

Theorem 0.6 and Corollaries 0.3, 0.4 could be generalized for operators of the form $D^M Q(D)$ and $Q(D)D^M$, where M is a positive integer.

We shall consider now indefinite and definite integrals for a right invertible operator.

Suppose that $D \in R(X)$. An element $y \in \mathscr{D}_D$ is said to be *primitive* for an $x \in X$ if $Dy = x$. It is easy to prove that the difference of two primitive elements is a *constant*, i.e. an element of the set Z_D, and that *every* primitive element for x is of the form: $y = Rx + z$, where $R \in \mathscr{R}_D$ is arbitrarily fixed and $z \in Z_D$ is arbitrary. Thus the set $\mathscr{R}_D x = \{Rx + z : z \in Z_D\}$ with $R \in \mathscr{R}_D$ arbitrarily fixed is an *indefinite integral* for an element $x \in X$.

We assume, as previously, that $\mathscr{R}_D = \{R_\gamma\}_{\gamma\in\Gamma}$ is a family of right inverses of an operator $D \in R(X)$ and that $\mathscr{F}_D = \{F_\gamma\}_{\gamma\in\Gamma}$ is the corresponding family of initial operators. We have:

$$F_\alpha F_\beta = F_\beta \quad \text{and} \quad F_\beta R_\alpha = R_\alpha - R_\beta \quad \text{for all } \alpha,\beta \in \Gamma$$

This implies

<u>Proposition 0.1</u>. $R_\alpha x - R_\beta x = z$ for an arbitrary $x \in X$, where z

is a constant ($\alpha, \beta \in \Gamma$).

Proposition 0.2. The operator $F_\beta R_\alpha - F_\alpha R_\gamma$ does not depend on the choice of R_γ and is equal to $F_\beta R_\alpha$ for all $\alpha, \beta, \delta \in \Gamma$.

By Proposition 0.2 we can write

$$I_\alpha^\beta = F_\beta R_\gamma - F_\alpha R_\gamma \quad \text{for all} \quad \alpha, \beta, \gamma \in \Gamma$$

This immediately implies that $I_\alpha^\beta = F_\beta R_\alpha$ for all $\alpha, \beta \in \Gamma$. Then

$$I_\alpha^\beta x = z, \text{ where } z \text{ is a constant, for all } \alpha, \beta \in \Gamma \text{ and } x \in X, \tag{0.8}$$

$$I_\beta^\alpha = -I_\alpha^\beta \quad \text{for all } \alpha, \beta \in \Gamma \tag{0.9}$$

$$I_\alpha^\delta + I_\delta^\beta = I_\alpha^\beta \quad \text{for all} \quad \alpha, \beta, \delta \in \Gamma \tag{0.10}$$

$$I_\alpha^\beta D = F_\beta - F_\alpha \quad \text{for all} \quad \alpha, \beta \in \Gamma. \tag{0.11}$$

Proposition 0.3. Let $x \in X$ be arbitrary and let y be a primitive element for x. Then $I_\alpha^\beta x = F_\beta y - F_\alpha y$ for all $\alpha, \beta \in \Gamma$.

Formulae (0.8)-(0.11) and Proposition 0.3 permit us to say that the element $I_\alpha^\beta x$ is a *definite integral* of x for every $x \in X$, $\alpha, \beta \in \Gamma$. In particular, Proposition 0.3 could be formulated as follows: A definite integral of an element $x \in X$ is a difference of initial values of an element y primitive for x and this difference is independent of the choice of y.

We shall indicate now some applications of the results obtained above. We point out that proving the invertibility of the operator

$I + \hat{Q}$ is exactly the same in several cases as proving that a Volterra integral equation of the second kind has a unique solution.

Example 0.1. Let $X = C[0,1]$, $D = d/dt$. Then the set Z_D consists of all constant functions. The operators defined by means of the equality: $(R_a x)(t) = \int_a^t x(s)ds$, where $0 \leqslant a \leqslant 1$, are right inverses of D such that $I - \lambda R_a$ is invertible for every scalar λ. Observe that $\dim Z_D = 1$. The family of initial operators induced by R_a is defined as follows: $(F_a x)(t) = x(a)$. Consider operators of the form:

$$(\hat{F}_a x)(t) = \int_a^1 m(s)\, x(s)ds / \int_a^1 m(s)ds \text{ for } x \in C[0,1],$$

$$a \in [0,1], m \in C[0,1],$$

$$\lambda F_a + (1-\lambda)\hat{F}_b,\ \lambda F_a + (1-\lambda)F_b,\ b \in [0,1],\ \lambda \text{ is a scalar.}$$

These are also initial operators, because they are the projections *onto* the space of constants. In several particular cases the corresponding right inverses have eigenvalues. Thus in these cases an initial value problem for polynomials in $D = d/dt$ with scalar coefficients is ill-posed (Corollary 0.4).

The Taylor Formula (0.3) applied to a function $x \in \mathscr{D}_{D^N} = C^{(N)}[0,1]$ gives a classical Taylor formula with a remainder in an integral form. In order to obtain remainders either in the Lagrange form or in the Cauchy form it is enough to apply the Darboux property of continuous functions by two different estimations, without any theorem about the intermediate value, like the Rolle, or Lagrange theorems.

Observe that $X = C[0,1]$ is a commutative linear ring with the usual multiplication of functions: $(xy)(t) = x(t)y(t)$ for $x,y \in X$, $t \in [0,1]$. The operator D satisfies the following condition: $D(xy) = xDy + yDx$ for $x,y \in \mathcal{D}_D = C^1[0,1]$. We point out that the restriction to the interval $[0,1]$ in this example is not essential. The same is valid for any interval $[a,b]$, and also for functions continuous on a half-axis or on the real line.

<u>Example 0.2.</u> Let $X = C(\Omega)$, where $\Omega = [0,1]\times[0,1]$, and $(Dx)(t,s) = \partial x(t,s)/\partial t$. Then the operators R_a defined by the equality: $(R_a x)(t) = \int_a^t x(u,s)du$, $0 \leqslant a \leqslant 1$ are right inverses of D (such that the operators $I-\lambda R_a$ are invertible for all scalars λ). Observe that $\dim Z_D = +\infty$. The induced family of initial operators is defined as follows: $(F_a x)(t,s) = x(a,s)$.

<u>Example 0.3.</u> (Difference operators). Let X be the space of all sequences $\{x_n\}$, n is an integer, and let $Dx = \{x_{n+1} - x_n\}$. Then the operators R_m defined by means of the equality: $R_m\{x_n\} = \{\Sigma_{k=m}^{n-1} x_k\}$, m is an integer, are right inverses of D, such that the operators $I - \lambda R_m$ are invertible for every scalar λ. Each of the induced initial operators F_m maps any element $\{x_n\}$ into a constant sequence $\{x_m\}$, i.e. $F_m x_n = x_m$ for all integers n. Using these definitions we can solve difference equations, for instance, of the form: $\Sigma_{k=0}^{N} P_k(n)x_{n+k} = y_n$, where n is an arbitrary integer, with either initial conditions: $x_{m+j} = y_m$ (m is a fixed integer, $j = 0,1,\ldots,N-1$) or with mixed boundary conditions: $x_{m+j} = y_m$

($m = p_o, \ldots, p_{N-1}$, where $p_o, \ldots, p_{N-1}$ are fixed integers, $j = 0,1, \ldots, N-1$).

<u>Example 0.4.</u> (The Darboux problem for hyperbolic equations). Let $X = C(\Omega)$, where $\Omega = [a,b]\times[a,b]$, $D = \partial^2/\partial t\partial s$. In this case $Z_D = \{x: x(t,s) = \phi(t)+\psi(s),\ \phi,\psi, \in C^1[a,b]\}$. The operators $R_{u,v}$ defined by the equality: $(R_{u,v}x)(t,s) = \int_u^t\int_v^s x(\xi,\eta)d\eta d\xi$, $a \leqslant u,\ v \leqslant b$, are right inverses of D such that the operators $I - \lambda R_{u,v}$ are invertible for all scalars λ. The induced family $\{F_{u,v}\}$ of initial operators is given by the formula: $(F_{u,v}x)(t,s) = x(u,s) + x(t,v) - x(u,v)$. Consider the hyperbolic equation:

$$\frac{\partial^2 x}{\partial t\partial s} = A(t,s)\,\frac{\partial x}{\partial t} + B(t,s)\,\frac{\partial x}{\partial s} + C(t,s)x + y(t,s)\ , \qquad (0.12)$$

where $A,B,C,y \in X$, with the initial conditions:

$$x(u,s) = x_0(s)\ ,\quad x(t,v) = x_1(t),\ \text{where } x_0,x_1 \in C[a,b],$$
$$x_0(v) = x_1(u)\ . \qquad (0.13)$$

This is the Darboux problem for Equation (0.12). Write:

$$(Hx)(t,s) = A(t,s)\,\frac{\partial x}{\partial t} + B(t,s)\,\frac{\partial x}{\partial s} + C(t,s)x(t,s)\ .$$

We can now rewrite Equation (0.12) and Condition (0.13) as follows:

$$(D - H)x = y\ , \qquad (0.14)$$

$$F_{u,v}x = y_o, \quad \text{where } y_o(t,s) = x_o(t) + x_1(s) - x_1(u). \quad (0.15)$$

Since the operator $I-R_{u,v}H$ is invertible, the problem (0.14)-(0.15) is well-posed and has a unique solution $x = (I - R_{u,v}H)^{-1}(R_{u,v}y + y_o)$.

<u>Example 0.5.</u> (The Cauchy problem for hyperbolic equations). Let $X = C(\Omega)$, where $\Omega = [0,a]\times[0,b]$ and let D be defined as above. We consider the Cauchy problem for Equation (0.12), i.e. we admit the following conditions:

$$(x,t,g(t)) = x_o(t), \quad x_t'(t,g(t)) = x_1(t),$$

where the given function $g \in C^1[0,a]$ is such that $g'(t) > 0$, $g(0) = 0$, $g(a) = b$, $x_o \in C[0,a]$, $x_1 \in C^1[0,a]$. The operator R defined by the equality: $(Rx)(t,s) = \int_{g^{-1}(s)}^{t}\int_{g(\xi)}^{s} x(\xi,\eta)d\eta d\xi$ is a right inverse of D. The induced initial operator F is then of the form: $(Fx)(t,s) = x(g^{-1}(s),s) + \int_{g^{-1}(s)}^{t} x_t'(u,g(u))du$. Let H be defined as in Example 0.4. We consider Equation (0.14) with the initial condition

$$Fx = y_o, \quad \text{where } y_o(t,s) = x_o(g^{-1}(s),s) + \int_{g^{-1}(s)}^{t} x_1(u)du. \quad (0.16)$$

Since the operator $I-RH$ is invertible, the problem (0.14)-(0.16) is well-posed and has a unique solution $x = (I - RH)^{-1}(Ry + y_o)$.

<u>Example 0.6.</u> (The Picard problem for hyperbolic equations). Let X and D be defined as in Example 0.5. Let $g \in C^1[0,a], g'(t) > 0$,

$g(0) = 0$, $g(a) = b$. We consider the Picard problem for Equation (0.12), i.e. we are looking for solutions of Equation (0.12) satisfying the conditions:

$$x(t,0) = x_o(t),\ x(g(s),s) = x_1(s),\ \text{where } x_o \in C^1[0,a],$$
$$x_1 \in C^1[0,b],\ x_o(0) = x_1(0).$$

We put $(R\,x)(t,s) = \int_{g(s)}^{t} \int_0^s x(u,v)\,dv\,du$. The operator R is a right inverse of D. The corresponding initial operator is defined as follows: $(Fx)(t,s) = x(g(s),s) + x(t,0) - x(0,0)$. Let H be defined as in Example 0.4. We consider Equation (0.14) together with the initial condition

$$Fx = y_o,\ \text{where } y_o(t,s) = x_o(t) + x_1(s) - x_o(0). \qquad (0.17)$$

Since the operator $I - RH$ is invertible, the problem (0.14)-(0.17) is well-posed and has a unique solution $x = (I - RH)^{-1}(Ry + y_o)$.

<u>Example 0.7.</u> (Functional-differential equations with delayed argument in a singular case). Consider the equation

$$x^{(N)}(t) + \sum_{k=0}^{N-1} [a_{k0}(t)x^{(k)}(t) + \sum_{j=1}^{M} a_{kj}(t)x^{(k)}(t-h_{kj}(t))]$$
$$= y(t) \qquad (0.18)$$

for $t > 0$, where $y, a_{kj}, h_{kj} \in X$, X is the linear space of all real (or complex) functions continuous for $t \geqslant 0$. We assume also that the functions h_{kj} are increasing, $h_{kj}(t) \leqslant t$ for $t > 0$ and

$h_{kj}(0) = 0$ $(k = 0,1,\ldots,N-1;\ j = 1,2,\ldots,M)$. Under these assumptions the initial set for Equation (0.18) is $E_o = \{0\}$. Hence no initial function is given. We should admit only that the values of the unknown function x and its derivatives are given at the point 0:

$$x^{(k)}(0) = b_k \quad (k = 0,1,\ldots,N-1). \tag{0.19}$$

We are not able to apply the "step by step" method for solving Equation (0.18) in the space under consideration. However, we can apply Corollary 0.3. Indeed, if we write

$$(Q_k x)(t) = a_{k0}(t)\, x(t) + \sum_{j=1}^{N-1} a_{kj}(t) x(t-h_{kj}(t))$$

$$(k = 0,1,\ldots,N-1),$$

$$Q_N = I\ ,\quad D = \frac{d}{dt}\ ,\quad Q(D) = \sum_{k=0}^{N-1} Q_k D^k\ ,\quad (Fx)(t) = x(0)\ ,$$

$$(Rx)(t) = \int_0^t x(s)ds\ ,\quad Q = \sum_{k=0}^{N-1} Q_k R^{N-k} \quad (x \in X)\ ,$$

we conclude that $D \in R(X)$, $R \in \mathscr{R}_D$, F is an initial operator for D corresponding to R and, by our assumptions, the operator $I + \hat{Q}$ is invertible in the space $C[0,t]$, where $T > 0$ is arbitrary. Thus, rewriting the problem (0.18)-(0.19) in the form of IVP for the operator $Q(D)$:

$$Q(D)x = y\ ,\quad FD^k x = b_k \quad (k = 0,1,\ldots,N-1)\ ,$$

we conclude that this problem is well-posed in every space $C[0,T]$ and its unique solution is $x = (I + Q)^{-1}(R^N y + \Sigma_{k=0}^{N-1} R^k b_k)$. After some standard calculations we can obtain this solution in an explicit form.

<u>Example 0.8.</u> (Boundary and initial value problems for polyharmonic equations). Suppose that $t = (t_1,\ldots,t_n)$, $s = (s_1,\ldots,s_n) \in \mathbb{R}^n$. Write: $|t-s| = [\Sigma_{i=1}^{n}(t-s)^2]^{1/2}$ Suppose that $\Omega \in \mathbb{R}^n$ is a domain with the closed boundary $S = \partial\Omega$ of Liapunov type. Consider the space $X = C(\overline{\Omega})$, where $\overline{\Omega} = \Omega \cup S$. The Laplace operator $\Delta = \Sigma_{i=1}^{n} \partial^2/\partial t_i^2$ is right invertible in the space X. Indeed, consider the Poisson equation $\Delta x = y$, $y \in X$ with the zero boundary condition of Dirichlet type: $x|_S = 0$. The solution of this problem is unique and of the form: $x = Ry$, where $(Ry)(t) = \lambda_n \int_\Omega G(t,s)\, y(s) d\Omega_s$, $G(t,s)$ is the Green function of the first kind for the operator Δ with respect to the domain Ω and $\lambda_2 = \pi/2$, $\lambda_n = -(1/2)(n-2)\pi^{-n/2}\Gamma(n/2)$ for $n \geqslant 3$. Thus the operator R is a right inverse of Δ. It is well-known that this operator has an eigenvalue, namely $\lambda = -1$. The space of constants is, by definition, $Z_\Delta = \{x \in C(\overline{\Omega}): \Delta x = 0 \text{ in } \Omega\}$, i.e. the space of all functions harmonic inside and continuous in its closure. The initial operator F for Δ corresponding to R is defined as follows: for every $x \in X$ we have $Fx = h$, where $h \in Z$ and $x|_S = h|_S$. Indeed, we have $F^2 = F$, $FX = Z_\Delta$ and $FR = 0$. Thus we can reduce (for instance) a boundary value problem for the biharmonic equation $\Delta^2 x = y$, $y \in X$, with the conditions: $\Delta x|_S = h_1$, $x|_S = h_o$, where $h_o, h_1 \in Z_\Delta$, to an initial value problem for right invertible operators. We conclude that this problem is well-posed and that its unique solution is

of the form: $x = R^2y + Rh_1 + h_o$. In a similar way we can consider an arbitrary polynomial in Δ with variable coefficients (even with sufficiently good operator coefficients). By a modification of the space under consideration we can obtain solutions of problems with Neumann boundary conditions and with different types of mixed boundary conditions.

1 Exponential, sine and cosine elements, D-polynomials

In the author's paper [7] exponential, cosine and sine elements have been defined. We recall here these definitions and some properties of these elements (cf. also the author [10]).

For simplicity only assume that X is a linear space over complexes.

Definition 1.1. If a number $\lambda \in \mathbb{C}$ is an eigenvalue of the operator $D \in R(X)$ then every eigenvector corresponding to the value λ is said to be an exponential element.

Proposition 1.1. Suppose that $D \in R(X)$, $\dim Z_D \neq 0$, $R \in \mathscr{R}_D$ and the operator $I-\lambda R$ is invertible for a $\lambda \in \mathbb{C}$. Then

(i) λ is an eigenvalue of the operator D and the corresponding eigenvectors are of the form

$$e_\lambda(z) = (I-\lambda R)^{-1}z, \quad \text{where } z \in Z_D \tag{1.2}$$

Moreover, the dimension of the eigenspace corresponding to the eigenvalue λ is equal to the dimension of the space of constants Z_D.

(ii) If $\lambda \neq 0$ then there exist non-trivial exponential elements $e_\lambda(z) \neq 0$.

(iii) If F is an initial operator for D corresponding to the operator R then exponential elements $e_\lambda(z)$ are uniquely determined by their initial values, i.e.

$$e_\lambda(z) = (I-\lambda R)^{-1} F[e_\lambda(z)], \text{ i.e. } F[e_\lambda(z)] = z \qquad (1.3)$$

(for the proof see the author [7]).

We recall that an operator $A \in L_0(X)$ is said to be a *Volterra operator* if the operator $I-\lambda A$ is invertible for every $\lambda \in \mathbb{C}$. The set of all Volterra operators belonging to $L_0(X)$ will be denoted by $V(X)$.

An immediate consequence of Property 1.1 is

Proposition 1.2. Suppose that $D \in R(X)$, $\dim Z_D \neq 0$, and that there is a right inverse R of D which is a Volterra operator. Then every scalar $\lambda \in \mathbb{C}$ is an eigenvalue of the operator D, i.e. for every $\lambda \in \mathbb{C}$ there exist non-trivial exponential elements.

The assumption in Proposition 1.2 that R is a Volterra operator is sufficient for the existence of non-trivial exponential elements, but not necessary, as will be shown in Examples 4.6 and 4.7.

Proposition 1.3. Suppose that $D \in R(X)$ and $R \in \mathscr{R}_D$. If X is a Banach space and R is quasi-nilpotent then R is a Volterra operator.

Proof: Suppose that λ is an arbitrary scalar, X is a Banach space and R is a quasi-nilpotent operator. Then the operator R is also quasi-nilpotent. Indeed,

$$\| \lambda^n R^n \|^{1/n} = |\lambda| \, \|R^n\|^{1/n} \to 0 \text{ as } n \to \infty.$$

Thus the operator $I-\lambda R$ is invertible and

$$(I-\lambda R)^{-1} = \sum_{k=0}^{\infty} \lambda^k R^k \tag{1.4}$$

(where the last series is convergent in the norm). The arbitrariness of λ implies that R is a Volterra operator.

<u>Proposition 1.4.</u> Suppose that $D \in R(X)$ and $R \in \mathscr{R}_D$. Then R is not a nilpotent operator.

Proof: Suppose that there exists a positive integer n such that R is a nilpotent operator of order n, i.e. we have

$$R^n = 0 \quad \text{and} \quad R^k \neq 0 \quad \text{for} \quad k = 0,1,2,\ldots,n-1.$$

Since $DR = I$, we find that $R^{n-1} = DR^n = 0$, which contradicts our assumption that R is nilpotent of order n.

Suppose that $D \in R(X)$ and $R \in \mathscr{R}_D$. A *D-polynomial of degree* n is an element of the form:

$$\sum_{k=0}^{n} R^k z_k, \quad \text{where} \quad z_0,\ldots,z_n \in Z_D \tag{1.5}$$

(cf. von Trotha [1]).

<u>Corollary 1.2.</u> Suppose that X is a Banach space, $D \in R(X)$, $\dim Z_S \neq 0$, $R \in \mathscr{R}_D$ and R is quasi-nilpotent. Then exponential elements exist and are of the form:

$$e_\lambda(z) = (I-\lambda R)^{-1} z = \sum_{k=0}^{\infty} \lambda^k R^k z, \; z \in Z_D, \; \lambda \in \mathscr{F}$$

i.e. are of the form of limits (in norm) of D-polynomials, where $z_k = \lambda^k z \in Z_D$ $(k = 0,1\ldots)$

<u>Definition 1.2.</u> Suppose that $D \in R(X)$, $\dim Z_D \neq 0$ and that there exists an $R \in \mathscr{R}_D \cap V(X)$. Operators

$$c_\lambda = \frac{1}{2}[e_{\lambda i} + e_{-\lambda i}];\ s_\lambda = \frac{1}{2i}[e_{\lambda i} - e_{-\lambda i}] \qquad \text{defined for all } \lambda \in \mathbb{C} \tag{1.7}$$

are called *cosine* and *sine operators*, respectively. Elements $c_\lambda(z)$ and $s_\lambda(z)$ defined for all $\lambda \in \mathbb{R}$, $z \in Z_D$ are called *cosine* and *sine elements*, respectively.

We have proved (cf. the author [10]) that cosine and sine elements have the following properties:

<u>Proposition 1.5.</u> Suppose that $D \in R(X)$, $\dim Z_D \neq 0$ and that there is an $R \in \mathscr{R}_D \cap V(X)$. Then for all $\lambda \in \mathbb{R}$

$$c_\lambda = (I+\lambda^2 R)^{-1},\quad s_\lambda = \lambda R(I+\lambda^2 R^2)^{-1}; \tag{1.8}$$

$$Dc_\lambda(z) = -\lambda s_\lambda(z),\quad Ds_\lambda(z) = \lambda c_\lambda(z) \quad \text{for all } z \in Z_D \tag{1.9}$$

Moreover

$$(D^2+\lambda^2 I)u = 0 \tag{1.10}$$

if and only if

$u = c_\lambda (z_0) + c_\lambda(z_1)$, where $z_0, z_1 \in Z_D$ are arbitrary. (1.11)

Theorem 1.1. Suppose that X is a commutative linear ring over $\mathbb{C}$, $D \in R(X)$, $\dim Z_D \neq 0$, $R \in \mathscr{R}_D \cap V(X)$ and D satisfies the *Leibniz condition*: $D(xy) = xDy + yDx$ for all $x, y \in \mathscr{D}_D$. Then for every $z_1, z_2 \in Z_D$ and $\lambda, \mu \in \mathbb{C}$ there exists a $z_3 \in Z_D$ such that $e_\lambda(z_1)e_\mu(z_2) = e_{\lambda+\mu}(z_3)$. Moreover, the *trigonometric identity* holds, i.e. for every $z \in Z_D$ and $\lambda \in \mathbb{C}$ there exists a $z_0 \in Z_D$

$$[c_\lambda(z)]^2 + [s_\lambda(z)]^2 = z_0 .$$

A similar theorem is true if D satisfies the *Duhamel condition*, i.e. $D(xy) = xDy$ for all $x, y \in \mathscr{D}_D$.

We have also

Proposition 1.6. Suppose that all assumption of Proposition 1.4 are satisfied. Then

(i) For arbitrarily fixed $\lambda \in \mathbb{R}$ and $z \in Z_D$ the elements $c_\lambda(z)$ and $s_\lambda(z)$ do not vanish simultaneously. Moreover,

$$c_0(z) = z, \; s_0(z) = 0. \tag{1.12}$$

(ii) For arbitrarily fixed $\lambda \in \mathbb{R}$ and $z \in Z_D$ the element $c_\lambda(z)$ is even with respect to λ and the element $s_\lambda(z)$ is odd.

Proof: (i) Suppose that there exist $\lambda \in \mathbb{R}$ and $z \in Z_D$ such that $z \neq 0$ and $c_\lambda(z) = 0$, $s_\lambda(z) = 0$. Property (1.9) implies the following equalities:

$$(I+\lambda^2R^2)^{-1}z = c_\lambda(z) = 0, \quad (I+\lambda^2R^2)^{-1}\lambda Rz = \lambda R(I+\lambda^2R^2)^{-1}z = \tag{1.13}$$

$$= s_\lambda(z) = 0.$$

1) Let $c_\lambda(z) = 0$. Suppose that $\lambda = 0$. Then the first of Formulae (1.12) implies that $z = c_0(z) = 0$, which contradicts our assumption that $z \neq 0$. Now, suppose that $\lambda \neq 0$. Then the first of Equalities (1.14) implies that $z = 0$, for the operator $(I+\lambda^2F^2)^{-1}$ is invertible. This also contradicts our assumption that $z \neq 0$.

2) Let $s_\lambda(z) = 0$. If $\lambda = 0$ then the first of Formulae (1.12) implies that $c_0(z) = z \neq 0$. Suppose that $\lambda \neq 0$. Then the second of Formulae (1.13) implies that $\lambda Rz = 0$. Since $\lambda \neq 0$, we find $Rz = 0$ and $z = DRz = 0$, which contradicts our assumption that $z \neq 0$.

(ii) Let $\lambda \in \mathbb{R}$ and $z \in Z_D$ be arbitrary. Equalities (1.8) imply that

$$c_{-\lambda}(z) = [I + (-\lambda)^2R^2]^{-1}z = (I+\lambda^2R^2)^{-1}z = c_\lambda(z),$$

$$s_{-\lambda}(z) = R[I + (-\lambda)^2R^2]^{-1}z = -\lambda R(I+\lambda^2R^2)^{-1}z = -s_\lambda(z).$$

This means that cosine elements are even and sine elements are odd with respect to λ.

Suppose that $D \in R(X)$ and $R \in \mathscr{R}_D$. Denote by $P(R)$ a linear space spanned on the set of all D-polynomials, i.e.

$$P(R) = \text{lin}\,\{R^k z : z \in Z_D,\ k \in \{0\} \cup \mathbb{N}\}. \tag{1.15}$$

Of course, $P(R) = \{0\}$ if and only if $\dim Z_D = 0$, since elements $R^K z$ $(k = 0,1,2,\ldots)$ are linearly independent (cf. the author [4]).

Suppose now that $R \in \mathscr{R}_D \cap V(X)$ and denote by $E(R)$ a linear space spanned on the set of all exponential elements, i.e.

$$E(R) = \text{lin}\,\{e_\lambda(z) : z \in Z_D,\ \lambda \in \mathbb{C}\}\ . \tag{1.16}$$

Since exponential elements $e_\lambda(z)$ and $e_\mu(z)$ are linearly independent for $\lambda \neq \mu$, we conclude that $E(R) = \{0\}$ if and only if $\dim Z_D = \{0\}$. Observe that, by definition,

$$c_\lambda(z) \in E(R),\quad s_\lambda(z) \in E(R) \quad \text{for all} \quad \lambda \in \mathbb{R}\ ,\quad z \in Z_D. \tag{1.17}$$

We have assumed (and we will assume) in all considerations concerning exponential elements that the considered right inverse is a Volterra operator. The reason was that exponential elements which are eigenvectors of the operator, were defined for all scalars λ. However, it is possible to restrict our considerations to the set E_{RV} of regular values of the operator R, provided that $\dim E_{RV} > 0$. In this case we shall define exponential elements for all $\lambda \in E_{RV}$. Further considerations proceed along similar lines.

2 Periodic operators and elements

Suppose that X is a linear space over $\mathbb{C}$ and that $D \in R(X)$. An operator $S \in L_0(X)$ is said to be *D-invariant* if

$$SD = DS \quad \text{on} \quad \mathcal{D}_D. \tag{2.1}$$

An operator $A \in L_0(X)$ is said to be *S-periodic* if there exists a D-invariant operator S such that

$$AS = SA\ . \tag{2.2}$$

Property 2.1. Suppose that $D \in R(X)$ and S is D-invariant. Then for arbitrary positive integer m

(i) the operator S^m is D-invariant;

(ii) if A is S-periodic then A is S^m-periodic.

Indeed, by an easy induction we show that Equality (2.1) implies

$$S^m D = DS^m \quad \text{on} \quad \mathcal{D}_D \quad (m = 1,2,\ldots), \tag{2.1'}$$

and that Equality (2.2) implies

$$AS^m = S^m A \quad (m = 1,2,\ldots)\ . \tag{2.2'}$$

Suppose we are given an arbitrarily fixed positive integer N and a D-invariant operator S. Write

$$X_{S,N} = x \in X : S^N x = x . \tag{2.3}$$

If $\dim X_{S,N} > 0$ then every element $x \in X_{S,N}$ will be called an S^N-*periodic element*. The definition of the space $X_{S,N}$ implies that the operator S is an involution of order N on the space $X_{S,N}$.* Thus we have (cf. the author [1], Chapter II)

$$X_{S,N} = \bigoplus_{j=1}^{N} X_j , \quad \text{where} \quad X_j = P_j X_{S,N} \quad \text{and}$$
$$P_j = \frac{1}{N} \sum_{k=0}^{N-1} \varepsilon^{-kj} S^k \quad (j = 1,\dots,N), \quad \varepsilon = e^{2\pi i/N} \tag{2.4}$$

Proposition 2.1. Suppose that S is a D-invariant operator and $\dim X_{S,N} > 0$ for $N > 1$. If $x_j \in X_j$ $(j = 1,2,\dots,N)$ then $Dx_j \in X_j$, where the spaces X_j are defined by Formulae (2.4).

Indeed, $x_j \in X_j$ if and only if $Sx_j = \varepsilon^j x_j$ (cf. the author [1], Chapter II). Thus $SDx_j = DSx_j = D(\varepsilon^j x_j) = \varepsilon^j Dx_j$ by Condition (2.1), which implies $Dx_j \in X_j$ $(j = 1,\dots,N)$.

Proposition 2.1 implies that each of spaces $X_1,\dots,X_n$ is invariant under the operator D. Hence the operator D *is invariant with respect to the decomposition* (2.4).

Proposition 2.2. Suppose that all assumptions of Proposition 2.1 are satisfied. Then $z \in Z_D$ implies $Sz \in Z_D$.

---

* cf. Muhamadiev [1], who has defined a p-periodic operator acting in a Banach space E as follows: a bounded linear operator U acting in E is said to be p-periodic if $U^p = I$ and $U^i x = x$ for $0 < i < p$ implies $x = 0$.

In other words: *A D-invariant operator preserves the space of constants.*

Indeed, if $s \in Z_D$, then $Dz = 0$. Hence Condition (2.1) implies that $DSz = SDz = 0$. Thus $Sz \in Z_D$.

Theorem 2.1. Suppose that $D \in R(X)$, $\dim Z_D \neq 0$ and $R \in \mathcal{R}_D \cap V(X)$. If an operator $S \in L_o(X)$ is D-invariant then for every $\lambda \in \mathbb{R}$ $z \in Z_D$ there exists $z_1 \in Z_D$ such that

$$Se_\lambda(z) = e_\lambda(z_1), \quad \text{where} \quad e_\lambda = (I - \lambda R)^{-1}, \tag{2.5}$$

i.e. the operator S *preserves the eigenspaces of the operator* D. One can say also that S *preserves all exponential elements up to a constant.*

Proof: By definition, $e_\lambda = (I - \lambda R)^{-1}$. Thus $(D - \lambda I)e_\lambda = (D - \lambda I)(I - \lambda R)^{-1} = D(I - \lambda R)(I - \lambda R)^{-1} = D$. Hence $De_\lambda = \lambda e_\lambda + D$ on $\mathcal{D}_D$. Condition (2.1) implies that $DSe_\lambda = SDe_\lambda = \lambda Se_\lambda + SD = \lambda Se_\lambda + DS$ for all scalars λ. Proposition 5.2 implies that for all $\lambda \in \mathbb{C}$ and for an arbitrary $z \in Z_D$ we have $DSe_\lambda(z) = \lambda Se_\lambda(z) + DSz = \lambda Se_\lambda(z) + Dz = \lambda Se_\lambda(z)$. We therefore conclude that the element $Se_\lambda(z)$ is also an eigenvector of D corresponding to the eigenvalue λ. Thus there exists a constant z_1 such that $Se_\lambda(z) = e_\lambda(z_1)$, which was to be proved.

Corollary 2.1. Suppose that all assumptions of Theorem 2.1 are satisfied. Then the constant z_1 in Formula (2.5) is defined by means of the equality

$$z_1 = FSe\,(z), \text{ where } F \text{ is an initial operator for } D \text{ corresponding to } R. \tag{2.6}$$

Kahane [1] has proved that every d/dt-invariant linear operator mapping each of the spaces $C[a,b]$ and $C^1[a,b]$ into itself is a constant multiple of the identity.

Theorem 2.2. Suppose that $D \in R(X)$, $S \in L_o(X)$ is a D-invariant operator, the operators $Q_{km} \in L_o(X)$ are S-periodic ($m = 0,1,\dots,M$; $k = 0,1,\dots,N-1$). Write

$$Q_m(S) = \sum_{k=0}^{N-1} Q_{km}S^k, \quad Q(D,S) = \sum_{m=0}^{M} Q_m(S)D^{m+M_1} \quad (M_1 \geqslant 0) \tag{2.7}$$

If $\dim X_{S,N} > 0$ for an $N > 1$ then

$$Q(D,S) = \sum_{j=1}^{N} Q(D,\varepsilon^j)P_j \quad \text{on} \quad X_{S,N}, \tag{2.8}$$

where the operators P_j are defined by decomposition (2.4).

Proof: Since the operators D and P_j ($j = 1,2,\dots,N$) commute, the decomposition (2.4) implies that for $j = 1,2,\dots,N$

$$\begin{aligned}
Q(D,S)P_j &= \sum_{m=0}^{M} Q_m(S)D^{m+M_1}P_j = \sum_{m=0}^{M} Q_m(S)P_jD^{m+M_1} = \\
&= \sum_{m=0}^{M} \left(\sum_{k=0}^{N-1} Q_{km}S^kP_j\right)D^{m+M_1} = \\
&= \sum_{m=0}^{M} \left(\sum_{k=0}^{N-1} \varepsilon^{jk}Q_{km}P_j\right)D^{m+M_1} = \\
&= \sum_{m=0}^{M} Q(\varepsilon^j)P_jD^{m+M_1} = \sum_{m=0}^{M} Q(\varepsilon^j)D^{m+M_1}P_j = Q(D,\varepsilon^j)P_j
\end{aligned}$$

Since $\Sigma_{j=1}^{N}P_j = I$, we finally obtain

$$Q(D,S) = Q(D,S) \sum_{j=1}^{N} P_j = \sum_{j=1}^{N} Q(D,S)P_j = \sum_{j=1}^{N} Q(D,\varepsilon^j)P_j .$$

Corollary 2.2. Suppose that all assumptions of Theorem 2.2 are satisfied. Then the equation

$$Q(D,S)x = y, \quad y \in X_{S,N} \tag{2.9}$$

is equivalent in the space $X_{S,N}$ to N independent equations

$$Q(D,\varepsilon^j)x_j = y_j; \quad \text{where } x_j = P_j x,\ Y_j = P_j Y \in X_j \quad (j = 1,\dots,N) \tag{2.10}$$

and the operators P_j and spaces X_j are defined by decomposition (2.4).

Proof: The definition of the operators P_j and elements x_j, y_j, $(j = 1,\dots,N)$ implies that $x = x_1 + \dots + x_N$, $y = y_1 + \dots + y_N$ and that this decomposition is uniquely determined. Since the operators Q_{km} are S-periodic, we have for $j = 1,\dots,N$; $k = 0,1,\dots,N-1$, $m = 0,1,\dots,M$: $SQ_{km}x_j = Q_{km}Sx_j = \varepsilon^j Q_{km}x_j$. Thus $Q_{km}X_j \subset X_j$. This implies that the operators $Q(D,\varepsilon^j)$ preserve all the spaces X_j. Indeed, if $x_j \in X_j$ then $Q(D,\varepsilon^j)x_j = \Sigma_{m=0}^{M} \Sigma_{k=0}^{N-1} Q_{km}D^{m+M_1}x_j \in X_j$ $(j = 1,\dots,N)$ by Proposition 2.1.

Hence Theorem 2.1 implies that

$$Q(D,S)x = Q(D,S) \sum_{j=1}^{N} P_j x = \sum_{j=1}^{N} Q(D,S)P_j x =$$

$$= \sum_{j=1}^{N} Q(D,\varepsilon^j)P_j x = \sum_{j=1}^{N} Q(D,\varepsilon^j)x_j .$$

Since $y = \Sigma_{j=1}^{N} P_j y = \Sigma_{j=1}^{N} y_j$ and since the space $X_{S,N}$ is a direct sum of spaces X_j $(j = 1,\ldots,N)$ and, moreover, $x_j, y_j \in X_j$ $(j = 1,\ldots,N)$, we conclude that the equation (2.9) is equivalent to the system (2.10).

Corollary 2.3. Suppose that all assumptions of Theorem 2.2 are satisfied. If each of equations (2.10) has a solution $x_j \in X_j$ $(j = 1,\ldots,N)$ then the equation (2.9) has a solution $x = x_1 + \ldots + x_N$ which is S^N-periodic. Conversely if the equation (2.9) has an S^N-periodic solution x, then j-th equation (2.10) has a solution $x_j = P_j \in X_j$, where the operator P_j is defined by decomposition (2.4) $(j = 1,\ldots,N)$.

Proof: If the equation (5.12) has an S^N-periodic solution then by definition $x \in X_{S,N}$. Hence $S^N x = x$ and $x = x_1 + \ldots + x_N$, where $x_j = P_j x \in X_j$ $(j = 1,\ldots,N)$. Corollary 2.2 implies that the equation (2.9) is equivalent to the system (2.10). Thus j-th equation (2.10) has a solution $x_j \in X_j$. Conversely, suppose that j-th equation (2.10) has a solution $x_j \in X_j$ $(j = 1,\ldots,N)$. Since $P_j^2 = P_j$, $P_j \neq P_k$ for $j \neq k$ and $x_j = P_j x$ for an $x \in X$ $(j,k = 1,\ldots,N)$ (cf. the author [3], Chapter III), writing: $x = x_1 + \ldots + x_N$ we find $P_j x = P_j \Sigma_{k=1}^{N} x_k = \Sigma_{k=1}^{N} P_j P_k x = P_j x = x_j$ $(j = 1,\ldots,N)$. Corollary 2.2 implies that $x \in X_{S,N}$ and that x is a solution of the equation (2.9).

Corollary 2.4. Suppose that all assumptions of Theorem 2.2 are satisfied and that $Q_M(S) = I$. Write

$$Q_j^o(R) = \sum_{m=0}^{M-1} Q_m(\varepsilon^j)R^{M_1-m} \quad \text{for} \quad R \in \mathscr{R}_D \ (j = 1,\ldots,N). \quad (2.11)$$

If there exists an operator $R \in \mathscr{R}_D$ such that $[I + Q^o(R)]X_j \subset X_j$ and the operators $I + Q_j^o(R)$ are invertible $(j = 1,\ldots,N)$ then

$$x = \sum_{j=1}^{N} x_j \in X_{S,N}, \quad \text{where}$$

$$x_j = R^{M+M_1} [I + Q^o(R)]^{-1} y_{M+M_1,j} + \sum_{k=0}^{M+M_1-1} R^k z_{jk},$$

$$y_{M+M_1,j} = y_j - \sum_{m=0}^{M-1} Q_{jm} \sum_{k=m}^{M-1} R^{k-m} z_{jm}, \quad z_{jk} \in Z_D \tag{2.12}$$

$$j = 1,\ldots,N;\ k = 0,1,\ldots,M+M_1-1)$$

The proof is an immediate consequence of the fact that the equation (2.9) is equivalent to the system (2.10) and that, by our assumptions, j-th equation (2.10) has a solution $x_j \in X_j$.

Corollary 2.5. Suppose that all assumptions of Corollary 2.4 are satisfied and that the operator D is invertible on the space $X_{S,N}$. Then the equation (2.9) has a unique solution

$$x = \sum_{j=1}^{N} x_j, \quad \text{where } x_j = R^{M+M_1} [I + Q_j^o(R)]^{-1}$$
$$(j = 1,\ldots,N),\ R = D^{-1}. \tag{2.13}$$

The proof follows immediately from Corollary 2.4 and from the fact that in our case $Z_D = \{0\}$. Hence all constants z_{jk} appearing in Formulae (2.12) vanish.

In a similar way as Theorem 2.2 and Corollaries 2.2-2.5 we

can consider the operator

$$Q(D,S) = D^{M_1} \sum_{m=0}^{M} Q_m(S) D^m .$$

In the case when the coefficients Q_{km} of the polynomials $Q_m(S)$ commute with D and S (for instance, are scalars) one can apply the above results directly.

In Section 6 conditions for the existence of periodic solutions of equations with right invertible operators will be given by means of R-shifts introduced in the next section.

3 R-shifts

In the sequel we shall write $A(\mathbb{R})$ instead of one of the sets: $\mathbb{R}$, $\mathbb{R}^+ = \{r \in \mathbb{R} : r \geqslant 0\}$.

<u>Definition 3.1.</u> Suppose that $D \in R(X)$, $\dim Z_D \neq 0$, and F is an initial operator for D corresponding to an $R \in \mathscr{R}_D$. Define a family $S_{A(\mathbb{R})} = \{S_h\}_{h \in A(\mathbb{R})} \subset L_o(X)$ of linear operators in the following way:

$$S_o = I \tag{3.1}$$

$$S_h R^k F = \sum_{j=0}^{k} \frac{(-1)^{k-j}}{(k-j)!} h^{k-j} R^j F \quad \text{for all } h \in A(\mathbb{R}), \quad k \in \{0\} \cup \mathbb{N}, \tag{3.2}$$

We say that the family $S_{A(\mathbb{R})}$ determines *R-shifts* for D and that S_h is an R-shift on h for an arbitrary $h \in A(\mathbb{R})$.

In particular, for $k = 0$ we have.

$$S_h F = F \quad \text{for all} \quad h \in A(\mathbb{R}) . \tag{3.3}$$

<u>Proposition 3.1.</u> Suppose that $D \in R(X)$, $\dim Z_D \neq 0$ and F is an initial operator for D corresponding to an $R \in \mathscr{R}_D$. Suppose that we are given a family $S_{A(\mathbb{R})} = \{S_h\}_{h \in A(\mathbb{R})}$ of R-shifts. Then for all $h \in A(\mathbb{R})$, $z \in Z_D$

$$S_h R^k z = \sum_{j=0}^{k} \frac{(-1)^{k-j}}{(k-j)!} h^{k-j} R^j z \quad (k = 0,1,2,\ldots) . \tag{3.4}$$

In particular,

$$S_h z = z \quad \text{for all} \quad z \in Z_D, \quad h \in A(\mathbb{R}) \tag{3.5}$$

i.e. *R-shifts preserve constants.*

Proof: Let $z \in Z_D$ be arbitrarily fixed. Then there exists an $x \in X$ such that $Fx = z$, for F is a mapping onto. Thus we have for all $h \in A(\mathbb{R})$

$$S_h R^k z = S_h R^k F x = \sum_{j=0}^{k} \frac{(-1)^{k-j}}{(k-j)!} h^{k-j} R^j F x =$$

$$= \sum_{j=0}^{k} \frac{(-1)^{k-j}}{(k-j)!} h^{k-j} R^j z .$$

Putting $k = 0$ we obtain Formula (3.5).

Theorem 3.1. Suppose that $D \in R(X)$, $\dim Z_D \neq 0$ and F is an initial operator for D corresponding to an $R \in \mathscr{R}_D$. Suppose that we are given a family $S_{A(\mathbb{R})} = \{S_h\}_{h \in A(\mathbb{R})}$ of R-shifts. Then

(i) If $A(\mathbb{R}) = \mathbb{R}^+$ then $S_{A(\mathbb{R})}$ is a commutative semigroup,

If $A(\mathbb{R}) = \mathbb{R}$ then $S_{A(\mathbb{R})}$ is an Abelian group, with respect to the superposition of operators, i.e.

$$S_{h_1} S_{h_2} = S_{h_2} S_{h_1} = S_{h_1+h_2} \quad \text{for all} \quad h_1, h_2 \in A(\mathbb{R}) .$$

(ii) For all $h \in A(\mathbb{R})$ the operators S_h are D-invariant and uniquely determined on the set P(R) (defined by means of Formula (1.15)).

(iii) If X is a complete linear metric space, $\overline{P(R)} = X$ and S_h are continuous for all $h \in A(\mathbb{R})$ then S_h are uniquely deter mined.

Proof: (i). Suppose that $A(\mathbb{R}) = \mathbb{R}^+$. Then for arbitrary $h_1, h_2 \in \mathbb{R}$ Definition 3.1 implies that

$$S_{h_1+h_2} R^k F = \sum_{j=0}^{k} \frac{(-1)^{k-j}}{(k-j)!} (h_1+h_2)^{k-j} R^j F = \sum_{m=0}^{k} (-1)^m (h_1+h_2)^m F^{k-m} F$$

$$= \sum_{m=0}^{k} \frac{(-1)^m}{m!} \sum_{j=0}^{m} \binom{m}{j} h_1^{m-j} h_2^j R^{k-m} F$$

$$= \sum_{j=0}^{k} \left(\sum_{m=j}^{k} \frac{(-1)^m}{(m-j)!} h_1^{m-j} R^{k-m} F \right) \frac{1}{j!} h_2^j$$

$$= \sum_{j=0}^{k} \left(\sum_{n=0}^{k-j} \frac{(-1)^{n+j}}{n!} h_1^n R^{k-n-j} F \right) \frac{1}{j!} h_2^j$$

$$= \sum_{j=0}^{k} \left(\sum_{n=0}^{k-j} \frac{(-1)^n}{n!} h_1^n R^{k-n-j} F \right) \frac{(-1)^j}{j!} h_2^j$$

$$= \sum_{j=0}^{k} \frac{(-1)^j}{j!} h_2^j S_{h_1} R^{k-j} F = S_{h_1} \sum_{j=0}^{k} \frac{(-1)^j}{j!} h_2^j R^{k-j} F$$

$$= S_{h_1} S_{h_2} R^k F .$$

Since we have $S_{h_2} S_{h_1} R^k F = S_{h_2+h_1} R^k F = S_{h_1+h_2} R^k F = S_{h_1} S_{h_2} R^k F$, we conclude that $S_{\mathbb{R}^+}$ is a commutative semigroup.

By the same arguments we conclude that $S_{\mathbb{R}}$ is an Abelian group.

(ii). Suppose that $0 \neq h \in A(\mathbb{R})$, $k \in \mathbb{N}$, $z \in Z_D$ are arbitrary fixed. Since $Dz = 0$, Proposition 3.1 implies that

$$(DS_h - S_hD)R^kz = DS_hR^kz - S_hDR^kz =$$

$$= D \sum_{j=0}^{k} \frac{(-1)^{k-j}}{(k-j)!} h^{k-j}R^jz - S_hR^{k-1}z =$$

$$= \frac{(-1)^k}{k!} Dz + \sum_{j=1}^{k} \frac{(-1)^{k-j}}{(k-j)!} h^{k-j}R^{j-1}z - \sum_{m=0}^{k-1} \frac{(-1)^{k-1-m}}{(k-1-m)!} h^{k-1-m}R^mz =$$

$$= \sum_{m=0}^{k-1} \left[\frac{(-1)^{k-1-m}}{(k-1-m)!} h^{k-1-m}R^mz - \frac{(-1)^{k-1-m}}{(k-1-m)!} h^{k-1-m}R^mz\right] = 0 ,$$

If $k = 0$, we have $(DS_h - S_hD)z = DS_hz - S_hDz = Dz = 0$. This implies that S_h, $h \in A(\mathbb{R})$, are D-invariant on the set $P(R)$. Definition 3.1 and Proposition 3.1 together imply that S_h are uniquely determined on the set $P(R)$.

(iii). Suppose that $h \in A(\mathbb{R})$ is arbitrarily fixed. The continuous operator S_h is, by Point (ii), uniquely determined on the set $P(R)$, which is dense in X by our assumption. Thus S_h is uniquely determined on the whole space X.

<u>Corollary 3.1.</u> Suppose that all assumptions of Theorem 3.1 are satisfied. Then

$$S_h^n = S_{nh} \quad \text{for all} \quad h \in A(\mathbb{R}),\ n \in \mathbb{N} \cup \{0\} . \tag{3.6}$$

This is an immediate consequence of Point (i) in Theorem 3.1.

<u>Corollary 3.2.</u> Let $X = C(\mathbb{R})$ be the space of all functions continuous on real line with the topology determined by the almost uniform convergence. Let $D = d/dt$, $(Rx)(t) = \int_0^t x(s)ds$, $(Fx)(t) = x(0)$, $(S_hx)(t) = x(t-h)$ for all $x \in X$, $h \in \mathbb{R}$. Then

S_h are unique continuous R-shifts acting in X, and for all assumptions of Theorem 3.1, Point (iii) is satisfied.

<u>Example 3.1.</u> Suppose that X, D, R, F, S_h are defined as in Corollary 4.2. Suppose, we are given a continuous function $g : \mathbb{R} \to \mathbb{R}$ such that $g'(t) > 0$ for $t \in \mathbb{R}$.* Write: $(Ax)(t) = x(g(t))$ for $x \in X$. Observe that by our assumptions the operator $A \in L_o(X)$ is invertible and $(A^{-1}y)(t) = y(g^{-1}(t))$ for $y \in X$, where g^{-1} denotes the inverse function for g. It is easy to see that $\hat{D} = DA \in R(X)$, $\hat{R} = A^{-1}R \in {}_D$, $\hat{F} = A^{-1}FA$, $Z_{\hat{D}} = \{A^{-1}z : z \in Z_D\} = A^{-1}Z_D$. Indeed, $\hat{D}\hat{R} = DAA^{-1}R = DR = I$, $\hat{F} = I - \hat{R}\hat{D} = I - A^{-1}RDA = A^{-1}(I - RD)A = A^{-1}FA$ and $\hat{D}\hat{z} = 0$ if and only if $\hat{z} = A^{-1}z$, where $z \in Z_D$. By our definitions we have

$$(\hat{R}x)(t) = (RAx)(t) = \int_o^{g^{-1}(t)} x(s)ds \quad \text{for} \quad x \in X, \tag{3.7}$$

$$\hat{z}(t) = z(g^{-1}(t)) \equiv c \in \mathbb{R} \quad \text{for} \quad z \in Z_D. \tag{3.8}$$

It is well-known that

$$(R^k z)(t) = c\,\frac{t^k}{k!} \quad \text{for} \quad z(t) \equiv c,\ k = 0,1,2,\ldots$$

Thus, by Formula (4.8),

---

*We can consider in the same manner the space $C(\mathbb{R}^+)$ of all functions continuous on the half-axis $\mathbb{R}^+$ with the topology determined by the almost uniform convergence and a continuous function $g : \mathbb{R}^+ \to \mathbb{R}^+$, such that $g'(t) > 0$ for $t \in \mathbb{R}^+$.

$$(\hat{R}^k\hat{z})(t) = c\,\frac{[g^{-1}(t)]^k}{k!} \quad \text{for } \hat{z}(t) \equiv c \quad (k = 0,1,2,\ldots)\,. \tag{3.9}$$

Write:

$$\gamma_h(t) = g(g^{-1}(t)-h) \quad \text{for } h \in \mathbb{R}. \tag{3.10}$$

$$(\hat{S}_h x)(t) = x(\gamma_h(t)) \quad \text{for } h \in \mathbb{R},\ x \in X. \tag{3.11}$$

We shall prove that $\hat{S}_{\mathbb{R}} = \{\hat{S}_h\}_{h\in\mathbb{R}}$ is a family of R-shifts. Indeed, let $k \in \mathbb{N} \cup \{0\}$ and $c \in \mathbb{R}$ be arbitrary and let $z(t) \equiv c$. Then we have

$$(\hat{S}_h R^k \hat{z})(t) = \sum_{j=0}^{k} \frac{(-1)^{k-j}}{(k-j)!} h^{k-j} (\hat{R}^j\hat{z})(t) =$$

$$= \sum_{j=0}^{k} \frac{(-1)^{k-j}}{(k-j)!} h^{k-j}\, c\, \frac{[g^{-1}(t)]^j}{j!} =$$

$$= \frac{c}{k!} \sum_{j=0}^{k} \frac{k!}{(k-j)!j!} (-1)^{k-j} h^{k-j} [g^{-1}(t)]^j =$$

$$= \frac{c}{k!} \sum_{j=0}^{k} \binom{k}{j} (-h)^{k-j} [g^{-1}(t)]^j = \frac{c}{k!} [g^{-1}(t)-h]^k =$$

$$= \frac{c}{k!} [g^{-1}(\gamma_h(t)]^k = (\hat{R}^k\hat{z})(u)\Big|_{u=\gamma_n(t)} = (\hat{S}_h\hat{R}^k\hat{z})(t),$$

which proves that $\hat{S}_h$ are $\hat{R}$-shifts $(h \in \mathbb{R})$. On the other hand, we have for $z \in Z_D$

$$(A^{-1}S_h R^k z)(t) = c\,\frac{[g^{-1}(t)-h]^k}{k!} \quad \text{for } z \in Z_D\,,$$

which implies

$$A^{-1}S_hR^kF = \hat{S}_h\hat{R}^kA^{-1}F \quad \text{for } h \in \mathbb{R} \quad (k = 0,1,2,\ldots).$$

We should point out that the function γ_h defined by means of Formula (4.11) is a general continuous solution of the so-called *translation equation* (cf. Moszner [1], [2], Moszner and Tabor [1]).

<u>Proposition 3.2.</u> Suppose that $D \in R(X)$, $\dim Z_D \neq 0$, F is an initial operator for D corresponding to $R \in \mathscr{R}_D$ and $S_{A(\mathbb{R})} = \{S_h\}_{h \in A(\mathbb{R})}$ is a family of R-shifts. Then

$$FS_hRFx = -hFx \quad \text{for all } x \in X,\ h \in A(\mathbb{R}). \tag{3.12}$$

Proof: By definition, $F^2 = F$ and $FR = 0$. Suppose that $x \in X$ and $h \in A(\mathbb{R})$ are arbitrarily fixed. Let $z = Fx$. Then $z \in Z_D$. Proposition 3.1 and Definition 3.1 together imply that $S_hRFx = S_hRz = Rz-hz$. Hence $FS_hRFx = F(RFx-hFx) = FRFx-hF^2x = -hFx$.

<u>Theorem 3.2.</u> Suppose that $D \in R(X)$, F is an initial operator for D corresponding to an $R \in \mathscr{R}_D$ and $S_{A(\mathbb{R})} = \{S_h\}_{h \in A(\mathbb{R})}$ is a family of D-invarient R-shifts. Write

$$F_n = FS_h^n\ ,\ D_n = D - \frac{1}{h}F_n \quad \text{for all } n \in \mathbb{N},\ h \in A(\mathbb{R}),\ h \neq 0. \tag{3.13}$$

Then $D_n \in R(X)$ and F_n is an initial operator for D and D_n, corresponding to the right inverse

$$R_n = R - F_nR = R - FS_h^nR \quad (n = 0,1,2,\ldots). \tag{3.14}$$

Moreover, if we consider the space of S_h^n-periodic elements:

$$X_{S_h,n} = x \in X : S_h^n x = x \ , \quad \dim X_{S_h,n} > 0 \quad (n \in \mathbb{N}) \tag{3.15}$$

then we have

$$F_n x = Fx \quad \text{for all} \quad x \in X_{S_h,n} \quad (n \in \mathbb{N}) \ . \tag{3.16}$$

Proof: Let $n \in \mathbb{N}$ and $h \in A(\mathbb{R})$ be arbitrarily fixed. Then F_n is a projection. Indeed, Formula 3.3 implies that $F_n^2 = FS_h^nFS_h^n = F^2S_h^n = FS_h^n = F_n$. Moreover, F_n is a projection *onto* the kernel Z_D of the operator D. Indeed, our assumptions and Formula 3.5 together imply that $F_nz = FS_h^nz = Fz = z$ for all $z \in Z_D$. Therefore F_n is an initial operator for D corresponding to the right inverse $R_n = R - F_nR = R - FS_h^nR$ (Theorem 2.4 of the author's paper [4]). The operator $D_n = D - \frac{1}{h} F_n$ is also right invertible, because we have $F_nR_n = 0$ (by definition) and $DF_n = DFS_h^n = 0$, which implies

$$D_nR_n = (D - \frac{1}{h} F_n)(R - F_nR) = DR - \frac{1}{h} F_nR - DF_nR + \frac{1}{h} F_n^2R =$$

$$= I - \frac{1}{h} F_nR + \frac{1}{h} F_nR = I.$$

Thus $R_n \in \mathscr{R}_{D_n}$ and F_n is an initial operator for D_n corresponding to the right inverse R_n.

Suppose now that $x \in X_{S_h,n}$, i.e. $S_h^n x = x$. Then $F_n x = FS_h^n x = Fx$, i.e. Equality (3.16) holds for $n \in \mathbb{N}$.

By definition of the operators D_n, F_n, R_n, we have the following identities:

$$D_n R_n = I \quad \text{on} \quad X_{S_h,n}, \; R_n D_n x = I - Fx \quad \text{on} \quad X_{S_h,n} \cap \mathscr{D}_D. \tag{3.17}$$

<u>Theorem 3.3.</u> Suppose that all assumptions of Theorem 3.2 are satisfied and that D_n, F_n, R_n, $X_{S_h,n}$ are defined by Formulae (3.13), (3.14), (3.15), respectively. Write:

$$X^{(m)}_{S_h,n} = X_{S_h,n} \cap \mathscr{D}_{D^m}, \; \hat{X}_{S_h,n} = \{x \in X_{S_h,n} : F_n Rx = 0\} \tag{3.18}$$

$$(n,m = 1,2,\dots)$$

Then the operator D_n maps $X^{(1)}_{S_h,n}$ into $X_{S_h,n}$, however the operator R_n maps $X_{S_h,n}$ onto $X^{(1)}_{S_h,n}$ and the following equalities hold

$$D_n x = Dx - \frac{1}{h} F_n x; \; D_n R_n = I, \; R_n D_n x = (I-F)x \quad \text{for} \tag{3.19}$$

$$x \in X^{(1)}_{S_h,n}, \; (n = 1,2,\dots)$$

Proof: Suppose that $n \in \mathbb{N}$, $h \in A(\mathbb{R})$ and $x \in X^{(1)}_{S_h,n}$ are arbitrarily fixed. Then $x \in \mathscr{D}_D$ and $S_h^n x = x$ and $y = D_n x = Dx - (1/h)F_n x = Dx - FS_h^n x = Dx - (1/h)Fx$. Since, by our assumptions, $S_h D = DS_h$ on the domain of D, we have $S_h^n D = DS_h^n$ on $\mathscr{D}_D$. This and Formula 3.3 together imply that

$$S_h^n y = S_h^n(Dx - \frac{1}{h} Fx) = DS^n x - \frac{1}{h} S_h^n Fx = Dx = \frac{1}{h} Fx = y ,$$

$$\text{i.e. } y \in X_{S_h,n} .$$

The arbitrariness of $x \in X_{S_h,n}^{(1)}$ implies that $D_n X_{S_h,n}^{(1)} \subset X_{S_h,n}$.

Suppose now that $x \in \hat{X}_{S_h,n}$ is arbitrarily fixed. Then $S_h^n x = x$ and $FS_h Rx = F_n Rx = 0$. Put $y = R_n x = Rx - FS_h Rx = Rx$. Since $D_n R_n = I$, we have $x = D_n R_n x = D_n y$. Thus $y \in \mathscr{D}_D$. Furthermore, $Fy = FR_n x = FRx - FF_n Rx = FRx = 0$ and $S_h^n y = S_h^n Rx$, i.e. $F_n y = FS_h^n y = FS_h^n Rx = F_n Rx$. Then $(I-F_n)y = y - F_n y = Rx - F_n Rx = R_n x = y$, which implies that $F_n y = 0$. But $x = S_h^n x = S_h^n Dy = DS_h^n y$. Then $S_h^n y = Rx + FS_h^n y = Rx + F_n y = Rx = y$, which implies that $y \in X_{S_h,n}^{(1)} = X_{S_h,n} \cap \mathscr{D}_D$. The arbitrariness of $X \in \hat{X}_{S_h,n}$ implies that $R_n \hat{X}_{S_h,n} \subset X_{S_h,n}^{(1)}$. We have obtained also $F_n x = FS_h x = Fx$ and $D_n x = Dx - (1/h)F_n x = Dx - (1/h)Fx$ and $R_n D_n x = (I-F_n)x = (I-F)x$ for $x \in X_{S_h,n}^{(1)}$.

<u>Example 3.2.</u> Suppose that $X = C[0,T]$, $D = d/dt$, $(Rx)(t) = \int_0^t x(s)ds$, $(Fx)(t) = x(0)$, $(Sx)(t+\omega) = x(t)$ for $x \in X$. Consider the space of all ω-periodic functions, i.e. the space $X_{S_h,1}$ for $(S_h x)(t) = x(t-\omega) = x(t)$. In a similar way, as it was shown in Corollary 3.1, we conclude that S_h is an R-shift on $h = -\omega$. It is easy to check that S_h is also a D-invariant R-shift. Examine the condition $FSR = 0$ which appears in Theorem 3.3. We have

$$(FS_hRx)(t) = F\left\{S_h\int_0^t x(s)ds\right\} = F\left[\int_0^{t+\omega} x(s)ds\right] = \left[\int_0^{t+\omega} x(s)ds\right]_{t=0} =$$

$$= \int_0^{\omega} x(s)ds \ .$$

We conclude that the condition $FS_hRx = 0$ in our case means that a definite integral on the period should vanish for some $x \in X_{S_h,1}$.

Observe that, by Formula (3.6), it is enough to consider in our further examination only the case $n = 1$.

<u>Proposition 3.3.</u> Suppose that all assumptions of Theorem 3.2 are satisfied. Suppose that $z \neq 0$ is an arbitrary constant. If $h \neq 0$ then $FS_hRz \neq 0$.

Indeed, if S_h is an R-shift on h then $FS_hRz = F(Rz-hz) = FRz - hFz = -hz \neq 0$.

Example 3.2 and Proposition 3.3 together show that the right inverses R_n introduced by means of Equality (4.14) are not the best ones for periodic problems. However, we have the following

<u>Theorem 3.4.</u> Suppose that $D \in R(X)$, $\dim Z_D \neq 0$, F is an initial operator for D corresponding to an $R \in \mathscr{R}_D$, and $S_{A(\mathbb{R})} = \{S_h\}_{h\in A(\mathbb{R})}$ is a family of D-invariant R-shifts. Suppose that operators D_1 and F_1 are defined by Formulae (3.13). Write:

$$R_1^o = R+F_1R + \frac{1}{h}RF_1R = (I+FS_h + \frac{1}{h}RFS_h)R \quad \text{for} \quad h \in A(\mathbb{R}). \tag{3.20}$$

Then the operator R_1^o maps the space $X_{S_h,1}$ onto the space $X^{(1)}_{S_h,1}$ and

$$D_1R_1^o = I \quad \text{on} \quad X_{S_h,1}, \; R_1^oD_1 = I \quad \text{on} \quad X_{S_h,1}^{(1)}, \tag{3.21}$$

i.e. the operator D_1 is invertible and its right inverse is $D_1^{-1} = R_1^o$. Moreover, an initial operator F_1^o corresponding to R_1^o vanishes on the space $X_{S_h,1}$.

Proof: Suppose that $h \in A(\mathbb{R})$ and $x \in X_{S_h,1}$ are arbitrarily fixed. Then $S_hx = s$, $F_1x = FS_hx = x$. Write: $z = F_1Rx = FS_hRx \in Z_D$. Since $DR = I$, $FR = 0$, we find

$$D_1R_1^ox = (D - \frac{1}{h} F_1)(R + F_1R + \frac{1}{h} RF_1R)x =$$

$$= (D - \frac{1}{h} F_1)(Rx + F_1Rx + \frac{1}{h} RF_1Rx) = (D - \frac{1}{h} F_1)(Rx + z + \frac{1}{h} Rz)$$

$$= DRx + Dz + \frac{1}{h} F_1Rx = \frac{1}{h} F_1z - \frac{1}{h^2} F_1Rz =$$

$$= x + \frac{1}{h} z - \frac{1}{h} z - \frac{1}{h} FS_hz = \frac{1}{h^2} FS_hRz =$$

$$= x - \frac{1}{h} Fz = \frac{1}{h^2} F(Rz-hz) = x - \frac{1}{h} z + \frac{1}{h} Fz = x - \frac{1}{h} z + \frac{1}{h} z = x.$$

The arbitrariness of $x \in X_{S_h,1}$ implies the first of Identities (3.21). Suppose now that $x \in X_{S_h,1}^{(1)}$ is arbitrarily fixed. Then $x \in \mathscr{D}_D$ and $S_hx = x$, $F_1x = FS_hx = FS_hx = Fx$ and

$$R_1^oD_1x = (R + F_1R + \frac{1}{h} RF_1R)(D - \frac{1}{h} F_1)x =$$

$$= (I + F_1 + \frac{1}{h} RF_1)R(Dx - \frac{1}{h} Fx) = (I + F_1 + \frac{1}{h} RF_1)(RDx - \frac{1}{h} RFx) =$$

$$= (I + FS_h + \frac{1}{h} RFS_h)(x - Fx - \frac{1}{h} RFx) =$$

$$= x - Fx - \frac{1}{h} RFx + FS_h x - FS_h Fx - \frac{1}{h} FS_h RFx +$$

$$+ \frac{1}{h} RFS_h x - \frac{1}{h} RFS_h Fx - \frac{1}{h^2} RFS_h RFx =$$

$$= x - fx - \frac{1}{h} RFx + Fx - F^2 x - \frac{1}{h} F(RFx - hFx) +$$

$$+ \frac{1}{h} RFx - \frac{1}{h} RF^2 x - \frac{1}{h^2} RF(RFx - hFx) =$$

$$= x - Fx - \frac{1}{h} FRFx + F^2 x - \frac{1}{h} RF^2 x - \frac{1}{h^2} RFRFx + \frac{1}{h} RF^2 x =$$

$$= x - Fx + Fx - \frac{1}{h} RFx + \frac{1}{h} RFx = x.$$

The arbitrariness of $x \in X^{(1)}_{S_h,1}$ implies the second of Identities (3.21). If we write $y = R_1 x$, we conclude that $y \in \overline{\mathscr{D}}_D$. Indeed, since $DF = 0$, we find $Dy = D(R + F_1 R + (1/h)RF_1 R)x = DRx + DFS_h Rx + (1/h)DRFS_h Rx = x + (1/h)FS_h Rx$. Moreover, $S_h y =$
$= S_h(I + F_1 + (1/h)RF_1)Rx = S_h Rx + S_h FS_h Rx + (1/h)RS_h RFS_h Rx =$
$= S_h Rx + FS_h Rx + (1/h)(RFS_h Rx - hFS_h Rx) = S_h Rx + FS_h Rx + (1/h)RFS_h Rx -$
$- FS_h Rx = S_h Rx + (1/h)RFS_h Rx$. Hence

$$u = y - S_h y = R_1^o x - (S_h Rx - \frac{1}{h} RFS_h Rx) = Rx + FS_h Rx + \frac{1}{h} RFS_h RX - S_h Rx +$$

$$+ \frac{1}{h} RFS_h Rx = Rx - S_h Rx + FS_h Rx$$

and $Du = D(y-S_h y) = DRx-DS_h Rx + DFS_h Rx = x-S_h DRx = x-S_h x = 0$, which implies that $u \in Z_D$. On the other hand, $Fu = FRx-FS_h Rx + F^2 S_h Rx = -FS_h Rx + FS_h Rx = 0$. We therefore conclude that $u = Fu = 0$, i.e. $S_h y = y$ and $y \in X^{(1)}_{S_h,1}$. The arbitrariness of $x \in X_{S_h,1}$ implies that $R^o_1 X_{S_h,1} \subset X^{(1)}_{S_h,1}$. An initial operator F^o_1 corresponding to R^o_1 is defined on $\mathscr{D}_{D_1}$ by the equality: $F^o_1 = I - R^o_1 D_1 = I - I = 0$.

Example 3.3. Suppose X, D, R. F. S are defined, as in Example 3.2. We shall show that

$$(R^o_1 x)(t) = \int_0^t x(s)ds + \left(\frac{t}{\omega} + 1\right) \int_0^\omega x(s)ds \text{ for } \omega\text{-periodic } x \in X. \tag{3.22}$$

Indeed, we have shown in Example 4.2 that $(FSRx)(t) = \int_0^\omega x(s)ds$. Hence

$$(RFS_h Rx)(t) = \int_0^t \left[\int_0^\omega x(u)du\right] ds = \left(\int_0^\omega x(s)ds\right)\left(\int_0^t dt\right) = t \int_0^\omega x(s)ds$$

and

$$(R^o_1 x)(t) = (Rx + FS_h Rx + \frac{1}{h} RFS_h Rx)(t) =$$

$$= \int_0^t x(s)ds + \int_0^\omega x(s)ds + \frac{t}{\omega} \int_0^\omega x(s)ds = \int_0^t x(s)ds + \left(\frac{t}{\omega}+1\right)\int_0^\omega x(s)ds$$

because we have for ω-periodic functions $x(t-h) = x(t+\omega) = x(t) = x(t-\omega)$, i.e. we can admit here $h = \omega$.

Theorem 3.5. Suppose that $D \in R(X)$, $\dim Z_D \neq 0$, F_o is an initial operator for an $R_o \in \mathscr{R}_D$ and $S_{A(\mathbb{R})} = \{S_h\}_{h\in\mathbb{R}}$ is a family of R_o-shifts. Suppose that $F \in L_o(X)$ is a projection onto the space Z_D of constants and that there exists a real d such that

$$FR_o^n z = \frac{d^n}{z!} z \quad \text{for all} \quad z \in Z_D \quad (n = 0,1,2,\ldots) . \tag{3.23}$$

Then F is an initial operator for D corresponding to the right inverse

$$R = R_o - FR_o , \tag{3.24}$$

and $\{S_{h-d}\}_{h\in\mathbb{R}}$ is a family of R-shifts.

Proof: Our assumptions and Theorem 2.4 of the author's paper [4] together imply that F is an initial operator for D corresponding to a right inverse R defined by means of Equality (2.4). We shall prove now that

$$R^n z = S_d R_o^n z \quad \text{for all} \quad z \in Z_D \quad (n = 0,1,2,\ldots) \tag{3.25}$$

Proof, by induction. Suppose that $z \in Z_D$ is arbitrarily fixed. If $n = 0$ we have $R^o z = z = S_d z = S_d R_o^o z$. Suppose Formula (3.25) to be true for an arbitrarily fixed $n \geqslant 0$. Then Formula (3.25) implies that

$$R^{n+1} z = R(R^n z) = R(S_d R_o^n z) = (R_o - FR_o) S_d R_o^n z =$$

$$= (R_o - FR_o) \sum_{j=0}^{n} \frac{(-1)^{n-j}}{(n-j)!} d^{n-j} R_o^j z =$$

$$= \sum_{j=0}^{n} \frac{(-1)^{n-j}}{(n-j)!} d^{n-j} (R_o^{j+1} z - FR_o^{j+1} z) =$$

$$= \sum_{j=0}^{n} \frac{(-1)^{n-j}}{(n-j)!} d^{n-j} \left(R_o^{j+1} z - \frac{d^{j+1}}{(j+1)!} z \right) =$$

$$= \sum_{j=0}^{n} \frac{(-1)^{n-j}}{(n-j)!} d^{n-j} R_o^{j+1} z - \sum_{j=0}^{n} \frac{(-1)^{n-j} d^{n+1}}{(n-j)!(j+1)!} z =$$

$$= \sum_{m=1}^{n+1} \frac{(-1)^{n+1-m}}{(n+1-m)!} d^{n+1-m} R_o^m z + \frac{d^{n+1}}{(n+1)!} \sum_{j=0}^{o} \frac{(-1)^{n+1-j}(n+1)}{(n-j)!(j+1)!} z =$$

$$= \sum_{m=1}^{n+1} \frac{(-1)^{n+1-m}}{(n+1-m)!} d^{n+1-m} R_o^m z + \frac{d^{n+1}}{(n+1)!} \sum_{j=0}^{n} \binom{n+1}{j+1} (-1)^{n+1-j} z =$$

$$= \sum_{m=0}^{n+1} \frac{(-1)^{n+1-m}}{(n+1-m)!} d^{n+1-m} R_o^m z - \frac{(-1)^{n+1}}{(n+1)!} d^{n+1} z +$$

$$+ \frac{d^{n+1}}{(n+1)!} \sum_{m=1}^{n+1} \binom{n+1}{m} (-1)^{n+2-m} z =$$

$$= S_d R_o^{n+1} z - \frac{d^{n+1}}{(n+1)!} \left[\sum_{m=1}^{n+1} \binom{n+1}{m} (-1)^{n+1-m} \right] z = S_d^{n+1} z$$

because the last sum vanishes. This proves Formula (3.25) for all non-negative integers. Having already proved this formula, we conclude from Point (i) of Theorem 3.1 that for arbitrary $z \in Z_D$, $h \in \mathbb{R}$ and non-negative integer n we have

$$S_{h-d} R^n z = S_d S_{h-d} R_o^n z = S_d \sum_{j=0}^{n} \frac{(-1)^{n-j}}{(n-j)!} (h-d)^{n-1} R_o^j z =$$

$$= \sum_{j=0}^{n} \frac{(-1)^{n-j}}{(n-j)!} (h-d)^{n-j} S_d R_o^j z = \sum_{j=0}^{n} \frac{(-1)^{n-j}}{(n-j)!} (h-d)^{n-j} R^j z$$

which proves that S_{h-d} are R-shifts.

<u>Remark 3.1.</u> Observe that an R-shift, in general is not an R^n-shift ($n = 2,3,4,\ldots$). Indeed, let $D \in R(X)$, $R \in \mathscr{R}_D$ and let S_h be an R-shift on $h \neq 0$. Write: $\hat{D} = D^2$. Then $z \in Z_D$ if and only if $\hat{z} = Rz_1+z_0$, where $z_1, z_0 \in Z_D$ are arbitrary. Thus we have:

$$S_h\hat{z} = S_h(Rz_1+z_0) = Rz_1-hz_1+z_0 = \hat{z}-hz_1 \neq \hat{z} \quad \text{if} \quad z_1 \neq 0.$$

<u>Example 3.4.</u> Suppose that $X_1,\ldots,X_n$ are linear spaces over $\mathbb{C}$, $D_j \in R(X_j)$, $\dim Z_{D_j} \in R(X_j)$, $\dim Z_{D_j} \neq 0$, $R_j \in \mathscr{R}_{D_j}$ ($j = 1,2,\ldots,n$). Suppose, moreover, that $S_h^{(j)}$ is an R_j-shift on $h \in A(\mathbb{R})$ ($j = 1, 2,\ldots,n$). Write:

$$X = X_1 \times \ldots \times X_n, \quad x = (x_1,\ldots,x_n) \in X$$

$$Dx = (D_1x_1,\ldots,D_nx_n), \quad Rx = (R_1x_1,\ldots,R_nx_n), \tag{3.26}$$

$$S_hx = (S_h^{(1)}x_1,\ldots,S_h^{(n)}x_n) \quad \text{for} \quad x \in X, \tag{3.27}$$

$$z = (z_1,\ldots,z_n) \in Z_D = Z_{D_1} \times \ldots \times Z_{D_n}. \tag{3.28}$$

It is easy to check that $D \in R(X)$, $R \in \mathscr{R}_D$, $\dim Z_D = \Sigma_{j=1}^n \dim Z_{D_j} \neq 0$ and that $\Sigma_{k=0}^n R^kz$ are D-polynomials. Moreover, for $k = 0,1,2,\ldots, z \in Z_D$ we have

$$\sum_{j=0}^{k} \frac{(n-1)^{k-j}}{(k-j)!} h^{k-j}R^jz =$$

$$= \sum_{j=0}^{k} \frac{(-1)^{k-j}}{(k-j)!} h^{k-j} (R_1^j z_1, \ldots, R_n^j z_n) =$$

$$= \left(\sum_{j=0}^{k} \frac{(-1)^{k-j}}{(k-j)!} h^{k-j} R_1^j z_1, \ldots, \sum_{j=0}^{k} \frac{(-1)^{k-j}}{(k-j)!} h^{k-j} R_n^j z_n \right) =$$

$$= (S_h^{(1)} R_1^k z_1, \ldots, S_h^{(n)} R_n^k z_n) = S_h (R_1^k z_1, \ldots, R_n^k z_n) = S_h R^k z \ ,$$

which proves that S_h is an R-shift on h.

Example 3.5. Suppose that X_j, D_j, R_j, $S_h^{(j)}$, X are defined, as in Example 3.4 and that $X_1 = \ldots = X_n$. Write:

$$D = [\delta_{jk} D_j]_{j,k=1,\ldots,n} \ , \ R = [\delta_{jk} R_j]_{j,k=1,\ldots,n} \ . \tag{3.29}$$

It is easy to verify that $D \in R(X)$, $R \in \mathscr{R}_D$ and $\dim Z_D \neq 0$. We shall prove that the operator

$$S_h = [\delta_{jk} S_k^{(j)}]_{j,k=1,\ldots,n}$$

is an R-shift on h. Indeed, for all $z \in Z_D$ and $m = 0,1,2,\ldots$ we have

$$S_h R^m z = [\delta_{jk} S_h^{(j)} R_j^m z_j]_{j,k=1,\ldots,n} =$$

$$= [\delta_{jk} \sum_{i=0}^{m} \frac{(-1)^{m-i}}{(m-i)!} h^{m-i} R_j^k z_{j,k=1,\ldots,n} =$$

$$= \sum_{i=0}^{m} \frac{(-1)^{m-i}}{(m-i)!} h^{m-i} [\delta_{jk} R_j^k z_j]_{j,k=1,\ldots,n} = \sum_{i=0}^{m} \frac{(-1)^{m-i}}{(m-i)!} h^{m-i} R^i z \ .$$

4 D-shifts

We shall determine now another class of shifts for right invertible operators by means of exponential operators e_λ defined by Formula (1.2).

Definition 4.1. Suppose that $D \in R(X)$, $\dim Z_D \neq 0$ and F is an initial operator for D corresponding to an $R \in \mathscr{R}_D \cap V(X)$. Define a family $S_{A(\mathbb{R})} = \{S_h\}_{h\in A(\mathbb{R})} \subset L_0(X)$ in the following way:

$$S_o = I, \tag{4.1}$$

and

$$S_h e_\lambda F = e^{-\lambda h} e_\lambda F \quad \text{for all} \quad h \in A(\mathbb{R}),\ \lambda \in \mathbb{C}. \tag{4.2}$$

We say that the family $S_{A(\mathbb{R})}$ determine *D-shifts* and that S_h is a D-shift on h for an arbitrary $h \in A(\mathbb{R})$.

In particular, for $\lambda = 0$ we have

$$S_h F = F \quad \text{for all} \quad h \in A(\mathbb{R}). \tag{4.3}$$

Proposition 4.1. Suppose that all assumptions of Definition 4.1 are satisfied and that $S_{A(\mathbb{R})} = \{S_h\}_{h\in A(\mathbb{R})}$ is a family of D-shifts. Then for all $h \in A(\mathbb{R})$, $z \in Z_D$

$$S_h e_\lambda(z) = e^{-\lambda h} e_\lambda(z). \tag{4.4}$$

In particular,

$$S_h z = z \quad \text{for all} \quad z \in Z_D,\ h \in \mathbb{R}\ , \tag{4.5}$$

i.e. *D-shifts preserve constants.*

Proof: Let $z \in Z_D$ be arbitrarily fixed. Then there is an $x \in X$ such that $Fx = z$. Thus we have for all $h \in A(\mathbb{R})$, $S_h e_\lambda(z) = S_h e_\lambda(Fx) = S_h e_\lambda Fx = e^{-\lambda h} e_\lambda Fx = e^{-\lambda h} e_\lambda(z)$. Putting $\lambda = 0$ we obtain Formula (4.5).

Theorem 4.1. Suppose that $D \in R(X)$, $\dim Z_D \neq 0$ and F is an initial operator for D corresponding to an $R \in \mathscr{R}_D \cap V(X)$. Suppose that we are given a family $S_{A(\mathbb{R})} = \{S_h\}_{h \in A(\mathbb{R})}$ of D-shifts. Then

(i) If $A(\mathbb{R}) = \mathbb{R}^+$ then $S_{A(\mathbb{R})}$ is a commutative semigroup, if $A(\mathbb{R}) = \mathbb{R}$ then $S_{A(\mathbb{R})}$ is an Abelian group with respect to the superposition of operators, i.e.

$$S_{h_1} S_{h_2} = S_{h_2} S_{h_1} = S_{h_1+h_2} \quad \text{for all} \quad h_1, h_2 \in A(\mathbb{R})$$

(ii) For all $h \in A(\mathbb{R})$ the operators are D-invariant and uniquely determined on the set $E(R)$ (defined by means of Formula (1.15)).

(iii) If X is a complete linear metric space, $\overline{E(X)} = X$ and S_h are continuous for all $h \in A(\mathbb{R})$ then S_h are uniquely determined.

Proof: (i). Suppose that $A(\mathbb{R}) = \mathbb{R}^+$. For arbitrary $h_1, h_2 \in A(\mathbb{R})$,

$\lambda \in \mathbb{C}$ and $z \in Z_D$ we find

$$S_{h_1} S_{h_2} e_\lambda(z) = S_{h_1} e^{-\lambda h_2} e_\lambda(z) = e^{-\lambda h_2} S_{h_1} e_\lambda(z) =$$

$$= e^{-\lambda h_2} e^{-\lambda h_1} e_\lambda(z) = e^{-\lambda h_1 + h_2} e_\lambda(z) .$$

We therefore conclude that a superposition of D-shifts on h_1 and h_2 is again a D-shift on h_1+h_2. The commutativity of the operators S_{h_1} and S_{h_2} follows from the commutativity of addition in $A(\mathbb{R})$. If $0 \neq h \in \mathbb{R}$ then the D-shift S_{-h} is an inverse operator for the D-shift S_h, for $S_h S_{-h} = S_{-h} S_h = S_{h-h} = S_o = I$. Thus $S_{\mathbb{R}^+}$ is a commutative semigroup. The same arguments shows that $S_{\mathbb{R}}$ is an Abelian group.

(ii). Suppose now that $0 \neq h \in A(\mathbb{R})$, $\lambda \in \mathbb{C}$, $z \in Z_D$ are arbitrarily fixed. Since $De_\lambda(z) = \lambda e_\lambda(z)$, Proposition 4.1 implies that

$$[DS_h - S_h D] e_\lambda(z) = De^{-\lambda h} e_\lambda(z) - S_h[\lambda e_\lambda(z)] =$$

$$= \lambda e^{-\lambda h} e_\lambda(z) - \lambda e^{-\lambda h} e_\lambda(z) = 0 .$$

Hence S_h are D-invariant on the set $E(R)$. Definition 4.1 and Proposition 4.1 together imply that S_h are uniquely determined on the set $E(R)$.

(iii). Suppose that $h \in A(\mathbb{R})$ is arbitrarily fixed. The continuous operator S_h is, by Point (ii), uniquely determined on the set $E(R)$, which is dense in X by our assumption. Thus S_h

is uniquely determined on the whole space X.

Corollary 4.1. Suppose that all assumptions of Theorem 4.1 are satisfied. Then

$$S_h^n = S_{nh} \quad \text{for all} \quad h \in A(\mathbb{R}),\ n \in \mathbb{N} \cup \{0\}\ . \tag{4.6}$$

This is an immediate consequence of Point (i) in Theorem 4.1.

Corollary 4.2. Suppose that X, D, R, F and S_h are defined as in Corollary 3.1. Then S_h are unique continuous D-shifts acting in X, for all assumptions of Point (iii) of Theorem 4.1 are satisfied.

Observe that a *D-invariant* D-shift on h is an operator such that the constant z_1 appearing in Theorem 2.1 is equal $e^{-\lambda h}z$ for all $z \in Z_D$ and $\lambda \in \mathbb{C}$: $z_1 = e^{-\lambda h}z$. Hence Corollary 2.1 immediately implies

Proposition 4.2. If S_h is a D-invariant D-shift on $h \in A(\mathbb{R})$ and F is an initial operator corresponding to the operator R then

$$FS_h e_\lambda(z) = e^{-\lambda h}z \quad \text{for all} \quad \lambda \in \mathbb{C},\ z \in Z_D\ .$$

Proposition 4.2 does not imply that $\dim Z_D = 1$. Namely we have

Proposition 4.3. There exists an operator $\hat{D} \in R(X)$ and a $\hat{D}$-invariant D-shift S_h on $h \in A(\mathbb{R})$ that $\dim Z_{\hat{D}} = n$, where n is an arbitrarily fixed positive integer.

Indeed, if $D \in R(x)$, $\dim Z_D = 1$ and S_h is a D-invariant D-shift on h, we can consider the space $Y = X^n$ $(n = 1,2,\ldots)$. Write: $x = (x_1,\ldots,x_n) \in Y$, $\hat{D}x = (Dx_1,\ldots,Dx_n)$, $S_h x = (S_h x_1,\ldots,S_h x_h)$, $Rx = (Rx_1,\ldots,Rx_n)$. It is easy to verify that $\hat{D}$ is a right invertible operator in the space Y, $\hat{R} \in \mathscr{R}_{\hat{D}} \cap V(Y)$, $\dim Z_{\hat{D}} = n$ and that $\hat{S}_h \hat{D} = \hat{D}\hat{S}_h$ on $\mathscr{D}_{\hat{D}}$. Write $\hat{e}_\lambda = (I - \lambda\hat{R})^{-1}$. Then $\hat{S}_h \hat{e}_\lambda(z) = (S_h e_\lambda(z_1),\ldots,S_h e_\lambda(z_n)) = (e^{-\lambda h} z_1,\ldots,e^{-\lambda h} z_n) = e^{-\lambda h}(z_1,\ldots,z_n) = e^{-\lambda h} z$ for all $\lambda \in \mathbb{C}$ and $z = (z_1,\ldots,z_n) \in \hat{Z}_D = Z_{\hat{D}^n}$. Thus the operator $\hat{S}_h$ is a $\hat{D}$-shift on h. On the other hand, it is well-known that there exists an operator D such that $\dim Z_D = 1$, namely the operator $D = d/dt$. A D-invariant D-shift for this operator is a usual shift on $h : (Sx)(t) = x(t-h)$.

<u>Proposition 4.4.</u> Suppose that all assumptions of Theorem 4.1 are satisfied. Then for all $h \in A(\mathbb{R})$, $h \neq 0$

(i) exponential elements $e_\lambda(z)$ are S_h-periodic for $\lambda = (2\pi i/h)k$, where k is an arbitrary integer

(ii) cosine and sine elements $c_\lambda(z)$ and $s_\lambda(z)$ are S_h-periodic for $\lambda = (2\pi/h)k$, where k is an arbitrary integer.

Proof: (i). Suppose that $\lambda = 2\pi i/h\ k$, k is an arbitrary integer. Since S_h is a D-shift on h, we find

$$S_h e_\lambda(z) = e^{-\lambda h} e_\lambda(z) = e^{(-2\pi ik/h)h} e_\lambda(z) =$$

$$= (e^{-2\pi i})^k e_\lambda(z) = e_\lambda(z) .$$

(ii). Suppose now that $\lambda = (2\pi/h)k$, k is an arbitrary we find

$$S_h c_\lambda(z) = S_h \frac{1}{2}(e_{\lambda i}+e_{-\lambda i}) = \frac{1}{2}[S_h e_{\lambda i}(z)+S_h e_{-\lambda i}(z)] =$$

$$= \frac{1}{2}[e^{(-2\pi ik/h)h} e_{\lambda i}(z)+e^{(2\pi ik/h)h} e_{-\lambda i}(z)] =$$

$$= \frac{1}{2}[(e^{-2\pi i})^k e_{\lambda i}(z)+(e^{2\pi i})^k e_{-\lambda i}(z)] = \frac{1}{2}[e_{\lambda i}(z)+e_{-\lambda i}(z)] = c_\lambda(z).$$

A similar proof for elements $s_\lambda(z)$.

Proposition 4.5. Suppose that $D \in R(X)$, $\dim Z_D \neq 0$, F is an initial operator for D corresponding to an $R \in \mathscr{R}_D \cap V(X)$ and that $S_{A(\mathbb{R})} = \{S_h\}_{h\in A(\mathbb{R})}$ is a family of D-shifts. Then for all $0 \neq h \in A(\mathbb{R})$

$$FS_h Re_\lambda(z) \neq 0 \quad \text{for} \quad \lambda \neq \frac{2\pi i}{h} k, \text{ k is an arbitrary integer.} \tag{4.7}$$

Proof: Let $0 \neq h \in A(\mathbb{R})$ and $\lambda \neq (2\pi i/h)k$ (k is an arbitrary integer) be arbitrarily fixed. Then

$$FS_h Re_\lambda(z) = FS_h[\frac{1}{\lambda} e_\lambda(z) - z] = \frac{1}{\lambda}[FS_h e_\lambda(z) - FS_h z] =$$

$$= \frac{1}{\lambda} \{F[e^{-\lambda h} e_\lambda(z)] = Fz\} = \frac{1}{\lambda}[e^{-\lambda h} Fe_\lambda(z) - z] =$$

$$= \frac{1}{\lambda}[e^{-\lambda h} z - z] = \frac{1}{\lambda}(e^{-\lambda h}-1)z \neq 0$$

by our assumptions.

Theorem 4.2. Suppose that X is a Banach space, $D \in R(X)$, $\dim Z_D \neq 0$, $R \in \overline{\mathscr{R}_D}$ and $\overline{P(R)} = X$. If the series $A(\lambda) = \sum_{k=0}^{\infty} \lambda^k R^k F$

is convergent (in the operator norm topology) for every $\lambda \in \mathbb{C}$ and if S_h is an R-shift on $h \in A(\mathbb{R})$ then

$$S_h A(\lambda) = e^{-\lambda h} A(\lambda) \quad \text{for} \quad \lambda \in \mathbb{C} .$$

Proof: Let $\lambda \in \mathbb{C}$ be arbitrary. Since S_h is an R-shift on h, we have by our assumptions:

$$S_h A(\lambda) = S_h \sum_{k=0}^{\infty} \lambda^k R^k F = \sum_{k=0}^{\infty} \lambda^k S_h R^k F = \sum_{k=0}^{\infty} \lambda^k \sum_{j=0}^{k} \frac{(-1)^{k-j}}{(k-j)!} h^{k-j} R^j F =$$

$$= \left[\sum_{j=0} \left(\sum_{k=j}^{\infty} \lambda^k \frac{(-1)^{k-j}}{(k-j)!} h^{k-j} \right) R^j \right] F = \sum_{j=0}^{\infty} \left(\sum_{m=0}^{\infty} \lambda^{j+m} \frac{(-h)^m}{m!} R^j \right] F =$$

$$= \left[\sum_{j=0}^{\infty} \left(\sum_{k=0}^{\infty} \lambda^m \frac{(-h)^m}{m!} \lambda^j R^j \right] F = \sum_{j=0}^{\infty} e^{-\lambda h} \lambda^j R^j F = e^{-\lambda h} \sum_{j=0}^{\infty} \lambda^j R^j F =$$

$$= e^{-\lambda h} A(\lambda)$$

<u>Theorem 4.3.</u> Suppose that X is a Banach space, $D \in R(X)$, $\dim Z_D \neq 0$, $R \in \mathscr{R}_D$ is quasi-nilpotent and $\overline{P(R)} = X$. Then an R-shift on $h \in A(\mathbb{R})$ is a D-shift on h. Conversely, a D-shift S_h on h is an R-shift on h.

Proof: Suppose that S_h is an R-shift on $h \in A(\mathbb{R})$. This means that equalities (3.1), (3.2) hold. Since the operator R is quasi-nilpotent, exponential operators e_λ exist for $\mathbb{C}$ and

$$e_\lambda F = (I-\lambda R)^{-1} F = \sum_{n=0}^{\infty} \lambda^n F^n F \quad \text{for} \quad \lambda \in \mathbb{C}$$

This, and Theorem 4.2 together imply that $S_h e_\lambda F = e^{-\lambda h} e_\lambda F$

for all $\lambda \in \mathbb{C}$ which proves that S_h is a D shift.

Suppose now that S_h is a D-shift. This and corollary 1.2 together imply that for every $z \in Z_D$, $\lambda \in \mathbb{C}$ we have

$$\sum_{m=0}^{\infty} \lambda^m S_h R^m z = S_h \sum_{m=0}^{\infty} \lambda^m R^m z = S_h e_\lambda(z) = e^{-\lambda h} e_\lambda(z) =$$

$$= \left(\sum_{m=0}^{\infty} \frac{(-1)^m}{m!} \lambda^m h^m\right)\left(\sum_{j=0}^{\infty} \lambda^j R^j\right) z = \sum_{m=0}^{\infty} \sum_{j=0}^{m} \frac{(-1)^{m-j}}{(m-j)!} \lambda^{m-j} h^{m-j}\, {}^{j}R^{j} z =$$

$$= \sum_{m=0}^{\infty} \lambda^m \left(\sum_{j=0}^{m} \frac{(-1)^{m-j}}{(m-j)!} h^{m-j} R^j z\right) .$$

If we compare coefficients of powers of λ, we conclude that

$$S_h R^m z = \sum_{j=0}^{m} \frac{(-1)^{m-j}}{(m.j)!} h^{m-j} R^j z \quad \text{for every } z \in Z_D \text{ and m}$$

$$m = 0,1,2,\ldots$$

This means that S_h is an R-shift on h.

Example 4.1. Suppose that $X = C[0,\infty)$ and $D = d/dt$. The operator D is right invertible in X and has a Volterra right inverse R of the form: $(Rx)(t) = \int_a^t x(s)s^{-1}ds$, $a > 0$. It is easy to verify that exponential elements for the operator D are of the form Ct^λ, where C is an arbitrary real number, λ is an arbitrary complex number. Define the operators S_h by means of the equality: $(S_h x)(t) = x(rt)$, where $r > 0$. Hence S_h is an operator of multiplication of argument by a number $r > 0$. Write: $h = -\ln r$. Since $S_h(Ct^\lambda) = C(rt)^\lambda = Cr^\lambda t^\lambda = C(e^{-h})^\lambda t^\lambda = Ce^{-\lambda h}t^\lambda = e^{-\lambda h}Ct^\lambda$, we find that S_h are d/dt-shifts on $h = -\ln r$. The operator S_h is also an

R-shift on h. Indeed, $z \in Z_D$ if and only if $z(t) \equiv c$, where $c \in \mathbb{R}$. By an easy induction we can prove that

$$(R^k z)(t) = c\,\frac{(\ln t - \ln a)^k}{k!} \quad (k = 0,1,2,\ldots) .$$

Thus we have for all $c \in \mathbb{R}$, $k = 0,1,2,\ldots$

$$(S_h R^k z)(t) = S_h[\tfrac{c}{k!}(\ln t - \ln a)^k] = \frac{c}{k!}[\ln(rt) - \ln a]^k =$$

$$= \frac{c}{k!}(\ln t - \ln a + \ln r)^k = \frac{c}{k!}\sum_{j=0}^{k}\binom{k}{j}(\ln r)^{k-j}(\ln t - \ln a)^j =$$

$$= c\sum_{j=0}^{k}\frac{1}{k!}\,\frac{k!}{(k-j)!\,j!}(-1)^{k-j}(-\ln r)^{k-j}(\ln t - \ln a)^j =$$

$$= \sum_{j=0}^{k}\frac{(-1)^{k-j}}{(k-j)!}h^{k-j}\,\frac{c}{j!}(\ln t - \ln a)^j = \sum_{j=0}^{k}\frac{(-1)^{k-j}}{(k-j)!}h^{k-j}(R^j z(t)$$

which proves that S_h is an R-shift on $h = -\ln r$.

However, there are R-shifts which are not D-shifts.

<u>Example 4.2.</u> Suppose that X is the complement of the space of all polynomials P(t) defined for $t \in \mathbb{R}$ in the norm

$$\|x\|_o = \sup_{t\in\mathbb{R}} e^{-\sqrt{|t|}}\,|x(t)| .$$

It is easy to see that X is a Banach space, the set P(R) of all polynomials is dense in X and there do not exist non-trivial exponential elements. Indeed, though the set P(R) is dense in X, nevertheless it does not generate all continuous functions. The usual shifts: $(S_h x)(t) = x(t-h)$ is a bounded D-invariant

R-shift in the space X, for

$$\| S_h x \|_o = \sup_{t\in\mathbb{R}^o} e^{-\sqrt{|t-h|}} |x(t-h)| \leq e^{\sqrt{|h|}} \sup_{t\in\mathbb{R}} e^{-\sqrt{|t|}} |x(t)| \leq$$

$$\leq e^{\sqrt{|h|}} \| x \|_o .$$

However, S_h is not a D-shift, for non-trivial exponential elements do not exist.

Remark 4.1. Observe that a D-invariant D-shift S_h ($h \in A(\mathbb{R})$) is not, in general, a D^n-shift ($n \in \mathbb{N}$). Indeed, let $\hat{D} = D^2$ and let S_h be a D-invariant D-shift on $h \neq 0$. Let $\lambda = 0$. Then $\hat{z} \in Z_{\hat{D}}$ if and only if $\hat{z} = Rz_1 + z_0$, where $z_0, z_1 \in Z_D$ are arbitrary (Compare Remark 3.1). We have $S\hat{D} = SD^2 = DS^2 = \hat{D}S$ on $\mathscr{D}_{\hat{D}}$. But $S_h\hat{z} = S_hRz_1 + S_hz_o = S_hRz_1 + z_0$ and $u = \hat{z} - S_hz = Rz_1 + z_0 - (S_hRz_1 + z_0) = Rz_1 - S_hRz_1$. Hence $Du = DRz_1 - DS_hRz_1 = z_1 - S_hDRz_1 = z_1 - S_hz_1 = 0$, which implies that $u \in Z_D$ and S_hRz_1 and $S_hRz_1 = Rz_1 - u$, where $u \in Z_D$. Therefore $u = -FSRz_1$ and, in general $u \neq 0$, hence $S_h\hat{z} \neq \hat{z}$, which contradicts to our assumption that S_h is a $\hat{D}$-shift (Formula (4.5)).

Example 4.3. Suppose that $X_1,\ldots,X_n$ are linear spaces over $\mathbb{C}$, $D_j \in R(X_j)$, $\dim Z_{D_j} \neq 0$, $R_j \in \overline{\mathscr{R}}_{D_j} \cap V(X_j)$ ($j = 1,2,\ldots,n$). Write: $e_\lambda^{(j)} = (I - \lambda R_j)^{-1}$ for $\lambda \in \mathbb{C}$ ($j = 1,2,\ldots,n$). Suppose, moreover that operators S_j are D_j-invariant D_j-shift on h $A(\mathbb{R})$, respectively, i.e. $D_jS_j = S_jD_j$ on $\overline{\mathscr{D}}_{D_j}$ ($j = 1,2,\ldots,n$) and

$$S_j e_\lambda^{(u)}(z_j) = e^{-\lambda h_j} e^{(j)}(z_j) \text{ for } \lambda \in \mathbb{C},\ z_j \in Z_{D_j} \quad (j = 1,2,\ldots,n).$$

Let X, D, R be defined by Formulae (3.25), (3.26) and let

$$Sx = (S_1x_1,\dots,S_nx_n) \quad \text{for} \quad x \in X$$

$$e_\lambda(z) = (e_\lambda^{(1)}(z_1),\dots,e_\lambda^{(n)}(z_n)) \text{ for } z = (z_1,\dots,z_n) \in Z_D =$$

$$= Z_{D_1} \times \dots \times Z_{D_n} .$$

It is easy to check, that $D \in R(X)$, $R \in \mathscr{R}_D \cap V(X)$, $\dim Z_D = \Sigma_{j=1}^n \dim Z_{D_j} \neq 0$ and that $e_\lambda(z)$ are exponential elements for D. Moreover, $SD = DS$ on $\mathscr{D}_D$ and

$$Se_\lambda(z) = (S_1e_\lambda^{(1)}(z_1),\dots,S_ne_\lambda^{(n)}(z_n)) = (e^{-h_1}e_\lambda^{(1)}(z_1),\dots,e^{-h_n}e_\lambda(z_n))$$

$$= e^{-\lambda h_1}\dots e^{-\lambda h_n}(e_\lambda^{(1)}(z_1),\dots,e_\lambda^{(n)}(z_n)) = e^{-\lambda(h_1+\dots+h_n)}e_\lambda(z)$$

for all $\lambda \in \mathbb{C}$ and $z \in Z_D$. We therefore conclude that the operator S is a D-invariant D-shift on $h = h_1+\dots+h_n$.

<u>Example 4.4.</u> Suppose that X_j, $X_1 = \dots = X_n$, X, D_j, R_j, S_j, $e_\lambda^{(j)}$ (jj= 1,...,n) are defined as in Example 4.3 and D, R are defined by Formulae (3.29). Write:

$$S = [\delta_{jk}S_j]_{j,k=1,\dots,n},\; e_\lambda = [\delta_{jk}e^{(j)}]_{j,k=1,\dots,n} .$$

It is easy to verify that $D \in R(X)$, $R \in \mathscr{R}_D$ $V(X)$, $\dim Z_D \neq 0$. $SD = DS$ on $\mathscr{D}_D$. Moreover, if $\lambda \in \mathbb{C}$, $z = (z_1,\dots,z_n) \in Z_D =$ $= Z_{D_1} \times \dots \times Z_{D_2}$ then for all $\lambda \in \mathbb{C}$, $z \in Z_D$ we have

$$Se_\lambda(z) = S[\delta_{jk}e_\lambda^{(j)}(z_j)]_{j,k=1,\dots,n} =$$

$$= [\delta_{jk}S_j e_\lambda^{(j)}(z_j)]_{j,k=1,\dots,n} = [\delta_{jk}e^{-\lambda h_j}e_\lambda^{(j)}(z_j)]_{j,k=1,\dots,n} =$$

$$= e^{-\lambda h_1}\dots e^{-\lambda h_n}[\delta_{jk}e_\lambda^{(j)}(z_j)]_{j,k=1,\dots,n} = e^{-\lambda(h_1+\dots+h_n)}e_\lambda(z).$$

Hence S is a D-invariant D-shift on $H = h_1 + \dots + h_n$.

Example 4.5. Suppose that X is the space (s) of all complex (or real) sequences $\{x_n\}$, $n \in \mathbb{N}$. Define the operator D as the *difference* operator: $D\{x_n\} = \{x_{n+1} - x_n\}$. The operator D is right invertible and its right inverse R is defined as follows:

$$R\, x_n = y_n, \quad \text{where } y_1 = 0,\ y_n = \sum_{j=1}^{n-1} x_j \quad \text{for} \quad n \geqslant 2.$$

The space Z_D of constants consists of all constant sequences:

$$Z_D = \Big\{\{z_n\}\colon z_n = c,\ c \in \mathbb{C},\ n \in \mathbb{N}\Big\}.$$

The initial operator F corresponding to R is: $F\{x_n\} = z_n$, where $z_n = x_1$ for all $n \in \mathbb{N}$.

Suppose that $z = \{z_n\} \in Z_D$ is arbitrarily fixed. Then $z_n = c$ for a $c \in \mathbb{C}$ and all $n \in \mathbb{N}$. By an easy induction we obtain

$$R^k z = c\{\tbinom{n-1}{k}\} \quad \text{for all} \quad z \in Z_D\ ,\ k \in \mathbb{N} \cup \{0\} \tag{4.8}$$

The arbitrariness of $z \in Z_D$ implies that $R^kF\{x_n\} = x_1\{\binom{n-1}{k}\}$ for all $\{x_n\}$ and $k \in \mathbb{N} \cup \{0\}$. We therefore define R-shifts

$\{S_h\}_{h \in \mathbb{R}}$ by means of the equality:

$$S_h R^k F\{x_n\} = \sum_{j=0}^{k} \frac{(-1)^{k-j}}{(k-j)!} h^{k-j} R^j F\{x_n\} = x_1 \sum_{j=0}^{k} \frac{(-1)^{k-j}}{(k-j)!} h^{k-j} \{\binom{n-1}{j}\}.$$

Finally, we have

$$S_h R^k F\{x_n\} = x_1 \left\{ \sum_{j=0}^{k} \frac{(-1)^{k-j}}{(k-j)!} h^{k-j} \binom{n-1}{j} \right\} \tag{4.9}$$

$$\text{for all } \{x_n\} \in X,\ k \in \mathbb{N} \cup \{0\},\ h \in \mathbb{R}.$$

One can prove that R is a Volterra operator and that

$$e_\lambda F\{x_n\} = (I-\lambda R)^{-1} F\{x_n\} = x_1\{(\lambda+1)^{n-1}\} \quad \text{for all } \lambda \in \mathbb{C},\ \{x_n\} \in X.$$

therefore can define D-shifts $\{\hat{S}_h\}_{h \in \mathbb{R}}$ by means of the equality:

$$\hat{S}_h e_\lambda F\{x_n\} = e^{-h} x_1\{(\lambda+1)^{n-1}\} \quad \text{for all } \lambda \in \mathbb{C},\ \{x_n\} \in X,\ h \in \mathbb{R}. \tag{4.10}$$

Observe that R-shifts S_h defined by means of Formula (4.9) and D-shifts $\hat{S}_h$ defined by means of Formula (4.10) are indeed different.

Example 4.6. Suppose that X is a commutative linear ring over $\mathbb{C}$ with the unit e, $D \in R(X)$ and D satisfies the *Leibniz condition*:

$$D(xy) = xDy + yDx \quad \text{for } x,y \in \mathscr{D}_D \tag{4.11}$$

Suppose, moreover, that F is a multiplicative initial operator for D corresponding to a right inverse R. One can prove* that R has the following properties:

$$Rz = z(Re) \quad \text{for all } z \in Z_D \tag{4.12}$$

$$R^n e = \frac{(Re)^n}{n!} \quad \text{for all} \quad n \in \mathbb{N} \cup \{0\} . \tag{4.13}$$

The arbitrariness of $z \in Z_D$ in Formula (4.12) and Formula (4.13) together implies that

$$R^n F = \frac{(Re)^n}{n!} F \quad \text{for all} \quad n \in \mathbb{N} \cup \{0\} . \tag{4.14}$$

We therefore can determine R-shifts $\{S_h\}_{h\in\mathbb{R}}$: for all $k \in \mathbb{N} \cup \{0\}$ we have

$$S_h R^k F = \sum_{j=0}^{k} \frac{(-1)^{k-j}}{(k-j)!} h^{k-j} R^j F = \sum_{j=0}^{k} \frac{(-1)^{k-j}}{(k-j)!} h^{k-j} \frac{(Re)^j}{j!} F =$$

$$= \frac{1}{k!} \sum_{j=0}^{k} \frac{(-1)^{k-j} h^{k-j} k!}{(k-j)!j!} (Re)^j F = \frac{1}{k!} \left[\sum_{j=0}^{k} \binom{k}{j} (-h)^{k-j} (Re)^j \right] F =$$

$$= \frac{1}{k!} (Re - he)^k F = \frac{1}{k!} [(R-hI)e]^k F .$$

We conclude that

$$S_h R^k F = \frac{1}{k!} [(R-hI)e]^k F \quad \text{for all } h \in \mathbb{R} , \ k \in \mathbb{N} \cup \{0\} \tag{4.15}$$

---

*This is a private communication of Dr. H. von Trotha.

i.e.

$$S_h R^k z = \frac{z}{k!} [(R-hI)e]^k \quad \text{for all } h \in \mathbb{R},\ k \in \mathbb{N} \cup \{0\},\ z \in Z_D \tag{4.16}$$

Suppose now that X is not only a linear ring but a Banach algebra. We shall show that exponential elements exist. Indeed, let $\lambda \in \mathbb{C}$ be arbitrarily fixed. Then, by Formula (4.13),

$$\left\| \sum_{n=0}^{\infty} \lambda^n R^n e \right\| = \left\| \sum_{n=0}^{\infty} \lambda^n \frac{(Re)^n}{n!} \right\| \leqslant \sum_{n=0}^{\infty} |\lambda|^n \frac{\|Re\|^n}{n!} = e^{|\lambda| \cdot \|Re\|} .$$

Thus the series $\Sigma_{n=0}^{\infty} \lambda^n R^n e$ is convergent. Write: $e^{\lambda Re} = \Sigma_{n=0}^{\infty} \lambda^n R^n e$. $\Sigma_{n=0}^{\infty} \lambda^n R^n e$. Then for all $z \in Z_D$, $\lambda \in \mathbb{C}$ we have $\Sigma_{n=0}^{\infty} \lambda^n R^n z =$ $= z\, e^{\lambda Re}$. For arbitrarily fixed $\lambda \in \mathbb{C}$, $z \in Z_D$ the element $x = z\, e^{\lambda Re}$ is an eigenvector for the operator D corresponding to the eigenvalue λ. Indeed, since $Dz = 0$, $De = 0$, we find

$$Dx = D[z\, e^{\lambda Re}] = (Dz)e^{\lambda Re} + zDe^{\lambda Re} = z\, D \sum_{n=0}^{\infty} \lambda^n R^n e =$$

$$= zDe + z \sum_{n=1}^{\infty} \lambda^n DR^n e = z\lambda \sum_{n=1}^{\infty} \lambda^{n-1} R^{n-1} e = z\lambda \sum_{n=0}^{\infty} \lambda^n R^n e =$$

$$= ze^{\lambda Re} = \lambda x.$$

Moreover, since $Fz = z$, $Fe = e$ and $FR = 0$, we have

$$Fx = F[z\, e^{\lambda Re}] = (Fz)(Fe^{\lambda Re}) = z \sum_{n=0}^{\infty} \lambda^n FR^n e = z \cdot Fe = z \cdot e = z$$

Hence, by definition, $x = ze^{\lambda Re}$ is an exponential element for D and we can write:

$$e_\lambda(z) = z\, e^{\lambda Re} \quad \text{for} \quad \lambda \in \mathbb{C},\ z \in Z_D\ . \tag{4.17}$$

The arbitrariness of $z \in Z_D$ permits us to rewrite Formula (4.17) as follows:

$$e_\lambda F = e^{\lambda Re} F \quad \text{for all} \quad \lambda \in \mathbb{C}. \tag{4.18}$$

We point out that in our case the operator D has eigenvectors for every $\lambda \in \mathbb{C}$, however we do not assume that R is a Volterra operator.

Having already defined exponential elements we can determine D-shifts $\{\hat{S}_h\}_{h\in\mathbb{R}}$: for all $\lambda \in \mathbb{C}$ we have

$$\hat{S}_h e_\lambda F = e^{-\lambda h} e_\lambda F = e^{-\lambda h} e^{\lambda Re} F = e^{\lambda(R-hI)e} F\ . \tag{4.19}$$

Formulae (4.16) and (4.19) together imply that for arbitrary $z \in Z_D$, $\lambda \in \mathbb{C}$, $h \in \mathbb{R}$ we have

$$S_h e_\lambda(z) = S_h[e^{\lambda Re} z] = S_h \sum_{k=0}^{\infty} \lambda^k R^k z = \sum_{k=0}^{\infty} \lambda^k S_h R^k z =$$

$$= z \sum_{k=0}^{\infty} \frac{\lambda^k}{k!} [(R-hI)e]^k = z\, e^{\lambda(R-hI)e} = \hat{S}_h\, e_\lambda(z)\ .$$

The arbitrariness of $z \in Z_D$ implies that in our case R-shifts S_h and D-shifts $\hat{S}_h$ coincide.

In the author's paper [2] there was shown (Theorem 3.4) that in any commutative linear ring X with unity, if the operator $D \in R(X)$ satisfies Condition (4.11) and $R \in V(X)$ then there exists an operator $R \in L_o(X)$ such that $DT - TD = I$, namely $Tx = x\,Re$ for all $X \in \mathscr{D}_D$. The assumption that $R \in V(X)$ is not necessary. Indeed, let $x \in \mathscr{D}_D$ be arbitrary. Then

$$(DT-TD)x = D(xRe) - (Re)(Dx) = (Dx)(Re) + xDRe - (Re)(Dx) = xe = x.$$

The arbitrariness of x implies $DT-TD = I$. Thus, as a consequence of Theorems 3.2. and 3.5, in the same paper we obtained the following result: If X is a complete linear metric space and a commutative linear ring (with respect to the same addition operation) and if $D \in R(X)$ satisfies the Leibniz condition (4.11), then D is not continuous. Moreover, if $X \neq Z_D$ then $X \neq Z_{P(D)}$ for all non trivial polynomials $P(t)$ with coefficients in $\mathbb{C}$ (i.e. for such $P(t)$ that $P(t) \neq 0$ and $P(t) \neq at$ for all $a \in \mathbb{C}$).

<u>Example 4.7.</u> Suppose that X is a commutative linear ring over $\mathbb{C}$. $D_i \in R(X)$, $\dim \ker D_i \neq 0$, the superposition $D = D_1D_2$ exists, F_i is an initial operator for D_i corresponding to $R_i \in \mathscr{R}_{D_i}$ $(i = 1,2)$ and $R_1R_2 = R_2R_1$ $(D_1 \neq D_2)$. We shall assume, in addi-addition, that the operators R_i have the following property: there exist elements $d_i \in Z_D$ such that $d_i \neq 0$ $(i = 1,2)$ and

$$R_i^k z_i = \frac{d_i^k}{k!}, \quad R_j d_i z = d_i R_j z \qquad (4.20)$$

for all $z_i \in Z_{D_i}$, $z \in Z_D$ $(i \neq j;\ i,j=1,2)$, $k \in \mathbb{N} \cup \{0\}$.

By our assumptions, $D \in R(X)$, $R = R_2R_1 = R_1R_2 \in \mathscr{R}_D$ and the initial operator F corresponding to R is of the form: $F = F_1$ $F = F_1 + R_1F_2D_1$. Moreover, $Z_D = z_1 + Rz_2 : z_i \in Z_{D_i}$ $(i=1,2)$. By an easy induction we conclude that for all $z \in Z_D$, $k \in \mathbb{N} \cup \{0\}$

$$R^kz = (R_1R_2)^k(z_1+R_1z_2) = R_1^kR_2^k(z_1 + R_1z_2) = R_2^kR_1^kz_1 + R_1^{k+1}R_2^kz_2 =$$

$$= R_2^k \frac{d_1^k}{k!} z_1 + R_1^{k+1} \frac{d_2^k}{k!} z_2 = \frac{1}{k!} (d_1^kR_2^kz_1 + d_2^kR_1^{k+1}z_2) .$$

The arbitrariness of $z \in Z_D$ implies the arbitrariness of $z_i \in Z_{D_i}$. Thus we have

$$R^kF = \frac{1}{k!} (d_1^kR_2^kF_1 + d_2^kR_1^{k+1}F_2) \quad \text{for all} \quad k \in \mathbb{N} \cup \{0\}. \quad (4.21)$$

We therefore can determine R-shifts $\{S_h\}_{h\in\mathbb{R}}$ in the following way: for all $h \in \mathbb{R}$, $k \in \mathbb{N} \cup \{0\}$, by Formula (4.21) we have:

$$S_hR^kF = \sum_{j=0}^{k} \frac{(-1)^{k-j}}{(k-j)!} h^{k-j}R^jF = \sum_{j=0}^{k} \frac{(-1)^{k-j}}{(k-j)!} \frac{h^{k-j}}{j!} (d_1^jR_2^jF_1 +$$

$$+ d_2^jR_1^{j+1}F_2) =$$

$$= \frac{(-1)^k}{k!} \sum_{j=0}^{k} \frac{(-1)^jh^{k-j}}{(k-j)!j!} (d_1^jR_2^jF_1 + d_2^jR_1^{j+1}F_2) =$$

$$= \frac{(-1)^k}{k!} \sum_{j=0}^{k} \binom{k}{j} (-1)^jh^{k-j}(d_1^jR_2^jF_1 + d_2^jR_1^{j+1}F_2) =$$

$$= \frac{(-1)^k}{k!} (hI - d_1R_2)^kF_1 + (hI - d_2R_1)^kR_1F_2 .$$

Finally, we have

$$S_h R^k F = \frac{(-1)^k}{k!}\,[(hI-d_1R_2)^k F_1 + (hI-d_2R_1)^k R_1F_2] \tag{4.22}$$

for all $h \in \mathbb{R}$, $k \in \mathbb{N} \cup \{0\}$.

Assume now that X is a Banach algebra and the operators R_1, R_2, F_1, F_2 are bounded. We shall prove that exponential elements exist. Indeed, for $i,j = 1,2$, $i \neq j$, $\lambda \in \mathbb{C}$ we have

$$\left\| \sum_{n=0}^{\infty} \lambda^n \frac{d_i^n}{n!} R_j^n \right\| = \sum_{n=0}^{\infty} |\lambda|^n \frac{\|d_i\|^n}{n!} \|R_j\|^n = e^{|\lambda|\cdot\|d_i\|\cdot\|R_j\|}$$

Write: $e^{\lambda d_i R_j} = \Sigma_{n=0}^{\infty} \lambda^n (d_i^n/n!) R_j^n$ for $\lambda \in \mathbb{C}$, $i \neq j$. Thus we have by Formula (4.21)

$$\sum_{n=0}^{\infty} \lambda^n R^n F = \sum_{n=0}^{\infty} \frac{\lambda^n}{n!} (d_1^n R_2^n F_1 + d_2^n R_1^{n+1} F_2) =$$

$$= \left(\sum_{n=0}^{\infty} \frac{\lambda^n}{n!} d_1^n R_2^n\right) F_1 + \left(\sum_{n=0}^{\infty} \frac{\lambda^n}{n!} d_2^n R_1^n\right) R_1F_2 =$$

$$= e^{\lambda d_1 R_2} F_1 + e^{\lambda d_2 R_1} R_1 F_2$$

Let $z_i \in Z_{D_i}$ be arbitrary and let $z = z_1 + R_1z_2$. Then we have $x = \Sigma_{n=0}^{\infty}\ {}^{n}R^n z = e^{\lambda d_1R_2} z_1 + e^{\lambda d_2R_1} R_1z_2$. On the other hand, arguing, as in Example 4.6, we have: $Dx = \lambda x$ and $Fx = z$. Thus the element x is an exponential element for D and we can write:

$$e_\lambda(z) = e^{\lambda d_1R_2} z_1 + e^{\lambda d_2R_1} R_1z_2 \quad \text{for } z = z_1 + R_1z_2 \in Z_D,\ \lambda \in \mathbb{C}. \tag{4.23}$$

Observe that also in this case we have defined exponential

elements $e_\lambda(z)$ for every $\lambda \in \mathbb{C}$ without assumptions that either R_1 or R_2 or $R = R_1R_2 = R_2R_1$ is a Volterra operator. The arbitrariness of $z_1 \in Z_{D_1}$, $z_2 \in Z_{D_2}$ implies that we can rewrite Formula (4.23) in the following way:

$$e_\lambda F = e^{\lambda d_1 R_2} F_1 + e^{\lambda d_2 R_1} R_1 F_2 \quad \text{for} \quad \lambda \in \mathbb{C}. \tag{4.24}$$

We therefore can determine D-shifts $\{\hat{S}_h\}_{h \in \mathbb{R}}$: for every $\lambda \in \mathbb{C}$ we have

$$\hat{S}_h e F = e^{-\lambda h} e F = e^{-\lambda h}(e^{\lambda d_1 R_2} F_1 + e^{\lambda d_2 R_1} R_1 F_2) =$$

$$= e^{\lambda(d_1 R_2 - hI)} F_1 + e^{\lambda(d_2 R_1 - hI)} R_1 F_2 =$$

$$= \sum_{n=0}^{\infty} \frac{\lambda^n}{n!} (d_1 R_2 - hI)^n F_1 + \sum_{n=0}^{\infty} \frac{\lambda^n}{n!} (d_2 R_1 - hI)^n R_1 F_2 =$$

$$= \sum_{n=0}^{\infty} \lambda^n \frac{(-1)^n}{n!} [(hI - d_1 R_2)^n F_1 + (hI - d_2 R_1)^n R_1 F_2] =$$

$$= \sum_{n=0}^{\infty} \lambda^n S_h R^n F = S_h \sum_{n=0}^{\infty} \lambda^n R^n F = S_h e_\lambda F \ .$$

Thus in our case R-shifts S_h and D-shifts $\hat{S}_h$ do coincide.

All assumptions admitted in this Example seem to be rather artificial. Consider then a case, where all these assumptions are satisfied.

Let

$$X = C(\Omega),\ \Omega = [0,T]\times[0,T],\ T > 0,\ D_1 = \frac{\partial}{\partial t}\ ,\ D_2 = \frac{\partial}{\partial s}\ ,$$

$$(R_1x)(t,s) = \int_0^t x(u,s)\,du, \quad (R_2x)(t,s) = \int_0^s x(t,v)\,dv,$$

$$(F_1x)(t,s) = x(0,s), \quad (F_2x)(t,s) = x(t,0), \quad D = \frac{\partial^2}{\partial t \partial s},$$

$$(Fx)(t,s) = x(t,0) + x(0,s) - x(0,0), \quad (Rx)(t,s) = \int_0^t\int_0^s x(u,v)\,dv\,du$$

for all $x \in X$. We have: $Z_D = \{\phi(t) + \psi(s) : \phi, \psi \in C^1[0,T]\}$. It is easy to verify that functions d_1, d_2 defined as follows: $d_1(t,s) \underset{t}{\equiv} s$, $d_2(t,s) \underset{s}{\equiv} t$, have all the required properties. We know that there exist R-shifts and D-shifts which are identical. Let $z(t,s) = \phi(t) + \psi(s)$, where $\phi, \psi \in C^1[0,T]$. Since

$$(R_2^n\phi)(t,s) = \frac{s^n}{n!}\phi(t), \quad (R_1^n\psi)(t,s) = \frac{t^n}{n!}\psi(s) \text{ for } n \in \mathbb{N} \cup \{0\},$$

we have for all $h \in \mathbb{R}$, $k \in \mathbb{N} \cup \{0\}$

$$[S_h e_\lambda(z)](t,s) = e^{-\lambda h}(e^{\lambda d_1 R_2}\phi + e^{\lambda d_2 R_1}R_1\psi)(t,s)$$

$$= e^{-\lambda h}\sum_{n=0}^{\infty}\frac{\lambda^n}{n!}(d_1^n R_2^n + d_2 R_1^{n+1})(t,s) =$$

$$= e^{-\lambda h}\sum_{n=0}^{\infty}\frac{\lambda^n}{n!}\left[\frac{t^n s^n}{n!}\phi(t) + \frac{s^n t^{n+1}}{(n+1)!}\psi(s)\right] =$$

$$= e^{-\lambda h}\sum_{n=0}^{\infty}\frac{(\lambda t s)^n}{(n!)^2}\left[\phi(t) + \frac{t}{n+1}\psi(s)\right].$$

Similarly, we have

$$(S_h R^k z(t,s)) = \frac{(-1)^k}{k!}\sum_{j=0}^{k}\binom{k}{j}(-1)^j h^{k-j}(d_1^j R_2^j\phi + d_2^j R_1^{j+1}\psi)(t,s) =$$

$$= \frac{(-1)^k}{k!} \sum_{j=0}^{k} \binom{k}{j} (-1)^j h^{k-j} [r^j \frac{s^j}{j!} \phi(t) + s^j \frac{t^{j+1}}{(j+1)!} \psi(s)] =$$

$$= \frac{(-1)^k}{k!} \sum_{j=0}^{k} \binom{k}{j} h^{k-j} \frac{(-ts)^j}{j!} [\phi(t) + \frac{t}{j+1} \psi(s)] =$$

$$= \sum_{j=0}^{k} \frac{(-h)^{k-j} (ts)^j}{(k-j)!(j!)^2} [\phi(t) + \frac{t}{j+1} \psi(s)] .$$

In order to find the form of $S_h x$ for an arbitrary $x \in X$ we should approximate this function either by polynomials $\Sigma R^k z_k$, $z_k \in Z_D$, or by exponentials.

5 Shifts and semigroups

Suppose that X is a linear space over $\mathbb{C}$.

<u>Definition 5.1.</u> Suppose that $D \in R(X)$, $\dim Z_D \neq 0$, F is an initial operator for D corresponding to an $R \in \mathscr{R}_D$ and that either $R \in V(X)$ and $Z_{A(\mathbb{R})} = \{S_h\}_{h \in A((R)}$ is a family of D-shifts or $S_{A(\mathbb{R})}$ is a family of R-shifts. A mapping H of R onto X is said to be *canonical* for $S_{A(\mathbb{R})}$ if

$$(Hx)(h) = \hat{x}(h), \quad \text{where} \quad \hat{x}(h) = FS_h x \quad \text{for all} \quad h \in A(\mathbb{R}), \quad x \in X. \tag{5.1}$$

The mapping H has the following obvious properties:

$$H \text{ is linear, i.e. } \widehat{\lambda x + \mu y} = \lambda\hat{x} + \mu\hat{y} \quad \text{for all } \lambda, \mu \in \mathbb{C}, \quad x, y \in X, \tag{5.2}$$

$$\hat{x}(0) = Fx \quad \text{for all} \quad x \in X; \tag{5.3}$$

$$\text{if } x, y \in X \quad \text{and} \quad x = y \quad \text{then} \quad \hat{x} = \hat{y}; \tag{5.4}$$

$$\text{if } x \in X \text{ is } S_h\text{-periodic then } \hat{x}(nh) = \hat{x}(0) \quad \text{for all } n \in \mathbb{N}. \tag{5.5}$$

Theorem 5.1. Suppose that X is a complete linear metric space, $D \in R(X)$, $\dim Z_D \neq 0$, F is an initial operator for D corresponding to an $R \in \mathscr{R}_D \cap V(X)$ and the set $E(R)$ of exponential elements is dense in X. Suppose that $S_{A(\mathbb{R})} = \{S_h\}_{h \in A(\mathbb{R})}$ is a family of D-shifts. Then the canonical mapping H separates points, i.e.

$$\hat{x} = \hat{y} \quad \text{if and only if} \quad x = y. \tag{5.6}$$

Proof: By Formula (5.4) the equality $x = y$ implies $\hat{x} = \hat{y}$. Thus it is enough to prove that $x \neq y$ implies $\hat{x} \neq \hat{y}$.

Recall that elements $e_\lambda(z_1)$, $e_\mu(z_2)$, where $z_1, z_2 \in Z_D$ are linearly independent for $\lambda \neq \mu$, even in the case $z_1 \neq z_2$. In order to prove that the mapping H separates points in the space X, we shall show that H separates exponential elements $x = e_\lambda(z)$ and $y = e_\mu(z)$, where $0 \neq z \in Z_D$ and

$$\lambda \neq \mu + \frac{2\pi i}{h} k, \quad \text{where } k \text{ is an arbitrary integer.} \tag{5.7}$$

Suppose that $\hat{x} = \hat{y}$. Then for all $h \in A(\mathbb{R})$ we have

$$0 = \hat{x}(h) - \hat{y}(h) = FS_h z - FS_h y = FS_h[e_\lambda(z)] - FS_h[e_\mu(z)] =$$

$$= F[e^{-\lambda h} e_\lambda(z) - e^{-\mu h} e_\mu(z)] = e^{-\lambda h} Fe_\lambda(z) - e^{-\mu h} Fe_\mu(z) =$$

$$= e^{-\lambda h} z_1 - e^{-\mu h} z_2 = e^{-\lambda h}(z - e^{(\lambda-\mu)h} z)$$

which implies $z = e^{(\lambda-\mu)h} z$. Since $z \neq 0$, we obtain $e^{(\lambda-\mu)h} = 1$

and $\lambda - \mu = (2\pi i/h)k$, where k is an integer, which contradicts our assumption (5.7). Therefore $\hat{x} = \hat{y}$ for $x = e_\lambda(z)$, $y = e_\mu(z)$, where $z \in Z_D, \lambda, \mu \in \mathbb{C}$ are arbitrary. Since the set E(R) is dense in X, we conclude that $\hat{x} \neq \hat{y}$ for all $x, y \in X$ such that $x \neq y$.

<u>Theorem 5.2.</u> Suppose that X is a complete linear metric space, $D \in R(X)$, $\dim Z_D \neq 0$, F is an initial operator for D corresponding to an $R \in \mathscr{R}_D$ and the set P(R) of all D-polynomials is dense in X. Suppose that $S_{A(\mathbb{R})} = \{S_h\}_{h \in \mathbb{R}}$ is a family of R-shifts. Then the canonical mapping H separates points, i.e. Condition (5.6) holds.

Proof: Similarly, as in the proof of Theorem 5.2, we have only to show that $x \neq y \Rightarrow \hat{x} \neq \hat{y}$. Recall that elements $R^k z_1$ and $R^m z_2$, where $z_1, z_2 \in Z_D$ are linearly independent for $m \neq k$, even in the case $z_2 = z_1$.

Write:

$$x = R^k z_1, \quad y = R^k z_2, \quad z_1 \neq z_2, \ z, \ z_2 \in Z_D$$

$k \in \mathbb{N} \cup 0$ is arbitrary fixed. Suppose that $\hat{x} = \hat{y}$. Then for all $h \in A(\mathbb{R})$, since $FR = 0$, we have

$$0 = \hat{x}(h) - \hat{y}(h) = FS_h x - FS_h y = FS_h R^k z_1 - FS_h R^k z_2 =$$

$$= FS_h R^k (z_1 - z_2) = F \sum_{j=0}^{k} \frac{(-1)^{k-j}}{(k-j)!} h^{k-j} R^j (z_1 - z_2) =$$

$$= \sum_{j=0}^{k} \frac{(-1)^{k-j}}{(k-j)!} h^{k-j} \; FR^j(z_1-z_2) = \frac{(-1)^k}{k!} h^k F(z_1-z_2) =$$

$$= \frac{(-1)^k}{k!} h^k(z_1-z_2)$$

which implies $z_1 = z_2$. But this contradicts our assumption that $z_1 \neq z_2$. Thus $\hat{x} \neq \hat{y}$. Since the set P(R) is dense in X we conclude that $\hat{x} \neq \hat{y}$ for arbitrary $x,y \in X$ such that $x \neq y$.

<u>Theorem 5.3.</u> Suppose that X is a Banach space, $D \in R(X)$, $\dim Z_D \neq 0$, F is a bounded initial operator for D corresponding to an $R \in \mathscr{R}_D \cap V(X)$, $S_{A(\mathbb{R})} = \{S_h\}_{h \in A(\mathbb{R})}$ is a strongly continuous semigroup* (group) of D-shifts. If D is an infinitesimal generator for $S_{A(\mathbb{R})}$ then $\hat{x} \in C^1(A(\mathbb{R}))$ for all $x \in \mathscr{D}_{\tilde{D}}$ and

$$\frac{d}{dh} \hat{x}(h) = (\widehat{Dx})(h) \quad \text{for all } x \in \mathscr{D}_D,\ h \in A(\mathbb{R}) . \qquad (5.8)$$

Proof: Suppose that D is an infinitesimal generator for $S_{A(\mathbb{R})}$. It means that

$$D = \lim_{r \to 0} \frac{1}{r} (S_r - I)x \quad \text{for all } x \in \mathscr{D}_D$$

---

*cf. Yosida [1]

Write $y = Dx$ for $x \in \mathscr{D}_D$. Then for all $h \in A(\mathbb{R})$, $|r| < \delta$

$$\left\| \frac{\hat{x}(h+r)-\hat{x}(h)}{r} - \hat{y}(h) \right\| = \left\| \frac{1}{r}(FS_{h+r}x - FS_h x) - FS_h y \right\| =$$

$$= \| FS_h[\frac{1}{r}(S_r - I)x - Dx] \| \leqslant$$

$$\leqslant \| F \| \cdot \| S_h \| \cdot \| \frac{1}{r}(S_r - I)x - Dx \| \to 0$$

since by our assumptions there are $M > 0$ and $\beta < +\infty$ such that $\| S_h \| \leqslant M e^{\beta h}$ for all $h \in A(\mathbb{R})$ (cf. Yosida [1]).
This implies that

$$\hat{y}(h) = \lim_{r \to 0} \frac{\hat{x}(h+r)-\hat{x}(h)}{r} = \hat{x}'(h) \quad \text{for all} \quad h \in A(\mathbb{R}),$$

i.e. $\hat{x}'(h) = FS_h Dx = (\widehat{Dx})(h)$ for all $x \in \mathscr{D}_D$ and $h \in A(\mathbb{R})$.

Theorem 5.4. Suppose that X is a linear metric space. $D \in R(X)$ $\dim Z_D \neq 0$, $R \in \mathscr{R}_D \cap V(X)$ and that $S_{A(\mathbb{R})} = \{S_h\}_{h \in A(\mathbb{R})}$ is a family of D-shifts. If A is an infinitesimal generator for $S_{A(\mathbb{R})}$ then the restriction of A to the set $E(R)$ of all exponential elements is equal to the restriction of D to $E(R)$:

$$D|_{E(R)} = A|_{E(R)} \ . \tag{5.9}$$

Proof: We recall that $S_{A(\mathbb{R})} = \{S_h\}_{h \in A(\mathbb{R})}$ is a semigroup (group) (Theorem 4.1, Point (i)). Observe that, by definition of exponential elements, we have

$$E(R) \subset \mathscr{D}_D , \tag{5.10}$$

Let $0 \neq \lambda \in \mathbb{C}$ and $0 \neq z \in Z_D$ be arbitrarily fixed. Since the multiplication of elements by scalars is continuous in our topology, we find

$$[\tfrac{1}{h}(S_h - I) - D]e_\lambda(z) = [\tfrac{1}{h}(e^{-\lambda h} - 1) - \lambda]e_\lambda(z) =$$

$$= \lambda\left(\frac{e^{-\lambda h} - 1}{\lambda h} - 1\right)e_\lambda(z) \to 0 \quad \text{as} \quad h \to 0 .$$

This means that the limit $\lim_{h\to 0} (1/h)(S_n - I)$ exists on the set $E(R)$ and is equal to D, which proves Formula (5.9).

<u>Theorem 5.5.</u> Suppose that X is a complete linear metric locally convex space, $D \in R(X)$ is closed, $\dim Z_D \neq 0$, $R \in \mathscr{R}_D \cap V(X)$, the set $E(R)$ of all exponential elements is dense in X and $S_{A(\mathbb{R})} = \{S_h\}_{h\in A(\mathbb{R})}$ is a strongly continuous semigroup (group) of D-shifts. Then D is an infinitesimal generator for $S_{A(\mathbb{R})}$ and $\overline{\mathscr{D}_D} = X$, more over $S_h D = DS_h$ for all $x \in \mathscr{D}_D$ and $h \in A(\mathbb{R})$, i.e. D-shifts S_h are D-invariant.

Proof: It is well-known that $S_{A(\mathbb{R})}$, as a strongly continuous semigroup, has a closed infinitesimal generator A and $\overline{\mathscr{D}_A} = X$. Theorem 5.4 implies that $D|_{E(R)} = A|_{E(R)}$. But $\overline{E(R)} = X$ and both, D and A are closed. Thus $D = A$ on $\mathscr{D}_D$. Since $\overline{E(R)} = X$. Formula (5.10) implies that $\overline{\mathscr{D}_D} = X$. We therefore conclude that D is an infinitesimal generator for $S_{A(\mathbb{R})}$ and $S_h D = DS_h$ for all $x \in \mathscr{D}_D$ and $h \in A(\mathbb{R})$.

Theorem 5.6. Suppose that X is a linear metric space, $D \in R(X)$, $\dim Z_D \neq 0$, $R \in \mathscr{R}_D$ and $S_{A(\mathbb{R})} = \{S_h\}_{h \in A(\mathbb{R})}$ is a semigroup (group) of R-shifts. If A is an infinitesimal generator for $S_{A(\mathbb{R})}$ then the restriction of A to P(R) is equal to the restriction of D to P(R):

$$D\big|_{P(R)} = A\big|_{P(R)}, \tag{5.11}$$

where, as before, we denote by P(R) the set of all D-polynomials.

Proof: Observe that by the definition of D-polynomials we have

$$P(R) \subset \mathscr{D}_D . \tag{5.12}$$

Let $k \in \mathbb{N} \cup \{0\}$ and $z \in Z_D$ be arbitrarily fixed. Since the multiplication of elements by scalar is continuous in our topology, we find

$$[\tfrac{1}{h}(S_h - I) - D]R^k z = \tfrac{1}{h}(S_h R^k z - R^k z) - DR^k z =$$

$$= \frac{1}{h}\left(\sum_{j=0}^{k} \frac{(-1)^{k-j}}{(k-j)!} h^{k-j} R^j z - R^k z\right) - R^{k-1} z =$$

$$= \frac{1}{h}\left(\sum_{j=0}^{k} \frac{(-h)^{k-j}}{(k-j)!} - R^k z\right) - R^{k-1} z =$$

$$= \frac{1}{h}\left(\sum_{j=0}^{k-1} \frac{(-h)^{k-j}}{(k-j)!} R^j z + R^k z - R^k z\right) - R^{k-1} z =$$

$$= \frac{1}{h} \sum_{j=0}^{k-1} \frac{(-h)^{k-j}}{(k-j)!} R^j z - R^{k-1} z = \sum_{j=0}^{k-1} \frac{(-h)^{k-1-j}}{(k-j)!} R^j z - R^{k-1} z =$$

$$= \sum_{j=0}^{k-2} \frac{(-h)^{k-1-j}}{(k-j)!} R^j z + R^{k-1} z - R^{k-1} z = h \sum_{j=0}^{k-2} \frac{(-h)^{k-2-j}}{(k-1)!} R^j z \to 0$$

as $h \to 0$.

This means that the limit $\lim_{h\to 0}(1/h)(S_h - I)$ exists on the set P(R) and is equal to D, which proves Formula (5.11).

Theorem 5.7. Suppose that X is a complete linear metric locally convex space, $D \in R(X)$ is closed, $\dim Z_D \neq 0$, $R \in \mathcal{R}_D$, the set P(R) of all D-polynomials is dense and in X and $S_{A(\mathbb{R})} = \{S_h\}_{h \in A(\mathbb{R})}$ is a strongly continuous semigroup (group) of R-shifts. Then D is an infinitesimal generator for $S_{A(\mathbb{R})}$ and $\overline{\mathscr{D}}_D = X$, moreover $S_h D = DS_h$ on $\mathscr{D}_D$ for all $h \in A(\mathbb{R})$, i.e. R-shifts S_h are D-invariant.

The proof proceeds along the same lines as the proof of Theorem 5.4 by means of an application of Theorem 5.6.

Theorem 5.8. Suppose that X is a Banach space, $D \in R(X)$ is closed, $\dim Z_D \neq 0$, $R \in \mathcal{R}_D$ is bounded, the set P(R) of all D-polynomials is dense in X and $S_{A(\mathbb{R})} = \{S_h\}_{h \in A(\mathbb{R})}$ is a family of R-shifts. If the operator R has the following property:

$$\| R^k \| \leqslant \frac{\| R \|^k}{k!} \quad \text{for all} \quad k \in \mathbb{N} , \qquad (5.13)$$

then S_h are bounded R-shifts and, moreover, there exists a constant $c > 0$ such that

$$\| S_h x \| \leqslant c\, e^{\| h \|} \| x \| \quad \text{for all} \quad x \in X \text{ and } h \in A(\mathbb{R}) . \qquad (5.14)$$

Proof: Write: $r = \|R\|$. Suppose that $z \in Z_D$ is arbitrarily fixed. Then we have for all positive integers k and $h \in A(\mathbb{R})$:

$$\|S_h R^k z\| = \left\| \sum_{j=0}^{k} \frac{(-1)^{k-j}}{(k-j)!} h^{k-j} R^j z \right\| \leqslant$$

$$\leqslant \sum_{j=0}^{k} \frac{|h|^{k-j}}{(k-j)!} \frac{r^j}{j!} \|z\| \leqslant$$

$$\leqslant \frac{\|z\|}{k!} \sum_{j=0}^{k} \frac{k!}{(k-j)!j!} |h|^{k-j} r^j = \frac{\|z\|}{k!} (|h| + r)^k \leqslant$$

$$\leqslant e^{|h|+r} \|z\|$$

By our assumptions, $\overline{P(R)} = X$

$$\|S_h x\| \leqslant e^{|h|+r} \|x\| = c\, e^{|h|} \|x\| \quad \text{for all} \quad x \in X ,$$

where $c = e^r$. We therefore conclude that S_h are bounded R-shifts satisfying the condition (5.14).

Example 5.1. Suppose that X is the space $C(\mathbb{R})$ of all functions continuous on real line, $D = d/dt$, $(Rx)(t) = \int_0^t x(s)ds$, $(Fx)(t) = x(0)$, $(Sx)(t) = x(t-h)$ for all $x \in X$, $h \in \mathbb{R}$. $\{S_h\}_{h \in \mathbb{R}}$ is a family of R-shifts and D-shifts simultaneously. Write:

$$\hat{D} = D^2, \ \hat{R} = R^2 . \qquad (5.15)$$

Then $\hat{D} \in R(X)$, $\hat{R}$ is a right inverse for $\hat{D}$, an initial operator $\hat{F}$ corresponding to $\hat{R}$ is of the form $\hat{F} = F + RFD$ and

$$Z_{\hat{D}} = \{\hat{z} = z_o + Rz_1 : z_o, z_1 \in Z_D\} = \{c_o + c_1 t : c_o, c_1 \in \mathbb{R}\}.$$

It is easy to check that all exponential elements for the operator $\hat{D}$ are of the form:

$$\hat{e}_\lambda(\hat{z}) = c_o \mathrm{ch}\sqrt{\lambda} t + \frac{c_1}{\sqrt{\lambda}} \mathrm{sh} \sqrt{\lambda} t =$$

$$= \frac{1}{2} [(c_o + \frac{c_1}{\sqrt{\lambda}})e^{\sqrt{\lambda} t} + (c_o - \frac{c_1}{\sqrt{\lambda}})e^{-\sqrt{\lambda} t})] . \tag{5.16}$$

for $\lambda \in \mathbb{C}$, $c_o, c_1 \in \mathbb{R}$. Observe that S_h are neither $\hat{R}$-shifts nor $\hat{D}$-shifts.

Define $\{\hat{S}_h\}_{h\in\mathbb{R}}$ as $\hat{R}$-shifts, then for all $k \in \mathbb{N} \cup \{0\}$, $h \in \mathbb{R}$ we have:

$$\hat{S}_h \hat{R}^k \hat{F} = \sum_{j=0}^{k} \frac{(-1)^{k-j}}{(k-j)!} h^{k-j} R^j F =$$

$$= \sum_{j=0}^{k} \frac{(-1)^{k-j}}{(k-j)!} h^{k-j} R^{2j} (F-RFD) =$$

$$= \sum_{j=0}^{k} \frac{(-1)^{k-j}}{(k-j)!} h^{k-j} (R^{2j} F + R^{2j+1} FD) .$$

Hence for all $k \in \mathbb{N} \cup \{0\}$, $\hat{z} = z_o + Rz_1, z_o, z_1 \in Z_D$, $h \in \mathbb{R}$ we find

$$\hat{S}_h \hat{R}^k \hat{z} = \sum_{j=0}^{k} \frac{(-1)^{k-j}}{(k-j)!} h^{k-j} (R^{2j} z_o + R^{2j+1} z_1) =$$

$$= \sum_{j=1}^{k} \frac{(-1)^{k-j}}{(k-j)!} h^{k-j} \left(c_o \frac{t^{2j}}{(2j)!} + c_1 \frac{t^{2j+1}}{(2j+1)!} \right) . \tag{5.17}$$

Thus $\hat{S}_h$ are well-determined R-shifts on the whole space X. Now we shall prove that $\hat{S}_h$ are $\hat{D}$-shifts, i.e. that

$$\hat{S}_h\hat{e}_\lambda(\hat{z}) = e^{-\lambda h}\hat{e}_\lambda(\hat{z}) \quad \text{for all} \quad \lambda \in \mathbb{C},\ h \in \mathbb{R},\ \hat{z} \in Z_{\hat{D}} \ . \tag{5.18}$$

Observe that X is a locally convex linear metric space with the topology induced by the countable family of pseudonorms

$$\|x\|_n = \sup_{|t|\leqslant n} |x(t)| \quad (n \in \mathbb{N}) \ .$$

The set P(R) of all polynomials is dense in X. The operator R is quasinilpotent with respect to each pseudonorm. This and Proposition 1.2 together imply that the operator R is a Volterra operator. Therefore the operator $\hat{R} = R^2$ is a Volterra operator for the operator

$$I - \lambda R^2 = (I - \sqrt{\lambda}\ R)(I + \sqrt{\lambda}\ R)$$

is invertible for all $\lambda \in \mathbb{C}$, the series $\Sigma_{n=0}^{\infty} \lambda^n R^{2n} = \Sigma_{n=0}^{\infty} \lambda^n \hat{R}^n$ is convergent in the operator topology induced by the given topology and, moreover,

$$\sum_{n=0}^{\infty} \lambda^n \hat{R}^n = (I - \lambda\hat{R})^{-1} \ . \tag{5.19}$$

The operators $\hat{S}_h$ are continuous in this topology.

Formulae (5.16), (5.17) and (5.19) together imply that for all $\lambda \in \mathbb{C}$, $h \in \mathbb{R}$, $\hat{z} \in Z_{\hat{D}}$ we have

$$e^{-\lambda h}\hat{e}_\lambda(\hat{z}) = e^{-\lambda h}(c_o \operatorname{ch}\sqrt{\lambda}t + \frac{c_1}{\sqrt{\lambda}} \operatorname{sh}\sqrt{\lambda}t) =$$

$$= \left(\sum_{m=0}^{\infty} \frac{(-\lambda h)^m}{m!}\right) [c_o \sum_{k=0}^{\infty} \frac{(\sqrt{\lambda} t)^{2k}}{(2k)!} + \frac{c_1}{\sqrt{\lambda}} \sum_{k=0}^{\infty} \frac{(\sqrt{\lambda} t)^{2k+1}}{(2k+1)]} \} =$$

$$= \sum_{n=0}^{\infty} \sum_{k=0}^{n} \frac{(-\lambda h)^{n-k}}{(n-k)!} [c_o \frac{\lambda^k t^{2k}}{(2k)!} + \frac{c_1}{\sqrt{\lambda}} \frac{\sqrt{\lambda}\ \lambda^k t^{2k+1}}{(2k+1)!}] =$$

$$= \sum_{n=0}^{\infty} \sum_{k=0}^{n} \frac{\lambda^{n-k} \lambda^k (-1)^{n-k} h^{n-k}}{(n-k)!} (c_o \frac{t^{2k}}{(2k)!} + c_1 \frac{t^{2k+1}}{(2k+1)!}) =$$

$$= \sum_{n=0}^{\infty} \lambda^n \sum_{k=0}^{n} \frac{(-1)^{n-k} h^{n-k}}{(n-k)!} (R^{2k} z_0 + R^{2k+1} z_1) =$$

$$= \sum_{n=0}^{\infty} \lambda^n \sum_{k=0}^{n} \frac{(-1)^{n-k} h^{n-k}}{(n-k)!} \hat{R}^k \hat{z} = \sum_{n=0}^{\infty} \lambda^n \hat{S}_h \hat{R}^n \hat{z} =$$

$$= \hat{S}_h \sum_{n=0}^{\infty} \lambda^n \hat{R}^n \hat{z} = \hat{S}_h (I - \lambda \hat{R})^{-1} \hat{z} = \hat{S}_h \hat{e}_\lambda (\hat{z}) .$$

This implies that $\hat{S}_h$ are not only $\hat{R}$-shifts but also $\hat{D}$-shifts.

Example 5.2. Suppose that X is the space $C(-\infty,\infty)$ of all functions bounded and uniformly continuous, and D,R,F are defined as in Example 5.1. Since all functions in the space under consideration are bounded there do not exist non-trivial D-polynomials and exponential elements. Thus R-shifts and D-shifts do not exist. However in the space X there is defined a strongly continuous semigroup $\{S_h\}_{h \in \mathbb{R}}$ defined by means of Gauss kernels:

$$(S_h x)(t) = \begin{cases} (2\pi h)^{1/2} \int_{-\infty}^{\infty} e^{-(t-s)^2/2h} x(s) ds & \text{for } h > 0 \\ x(t) & \text{for } h = 0 \end{cases}$$

(cf. Yosida [1], section IX. 5, Example 2). The infinitesimal generator for this semigroup is the operator

$$A = \frac{1}{2} \frac{d^2}{dt^2} = \frac{1}{2} \hat{D} .$$

6 Existence of periodic solutions

In this section we shall look for periodic solutions of equations with periodic coefficients.

Theorem 6.1. Suppose that $D \in R(X)$, $\dim Z_D \neq 0$, F is an initial operator for D corresponding to an $R \in \mathscr{R}_D$ and $S_h \in L_o(x)$ is a D-invariant R-shift on $h \neq 0$. Then the equation

$$Dx = y,\ y \in X_{S_h,1} \tag{6.1}$$

(cf. Formula (3.14)) with the initial condition

$$Fx = x_o\ ,\quad x_o \in Z_D \tag{6.2}$$

has a unique S_h-periodic solution which is of the form

$$x = (I + FS_h + \frac{1}{h} RFS_h)Ry + x_o\ .$$

Proof: Let D_1, F_1, R_1^o be defined by Formulae (3.13) and (3.20). We are looking for S_h-periodic solutions of the problem (6.1)-(6.2), i.e. for such x that $S_hx = x$ and $F_1x = Fx = x_o$. Since $x_o \in Z_D$ and S_h is an R-shift on h, Theorem 3.3. implies that

$$x = R_1^oD_1x = R_1^o(Dx - \frac{1}{h} F_1x) = R_1^o(y - \frac{1}{h} Fx) = R_1^o(y - \frac{1}{h} x_o) =$$

$$= (R + FS_hR + \frac{1}{h} RFS_hR)(y - \frac{1}{h} x_o) =$$

$$= (I + FS_h + \frac{1}{h} RFS_h)Ry - \frac{1}{h}(Rx_o + FS_hRx_o + \frac{1}{h} RFS_hRx_o) =$$

$$= (I + FS_h + \frac{1}{h} RFS_h)Ry - \frac{1}{h}[Rx_o + F(Rx_o - hx_o) + \frac{1}{h} RF(Rx_o - hx_o)] =$$

$$= (I + FS_h + \frac{1}{h} RFS_h)Ry - \frac{1}{h} [Rx_o + FRx_o - hFx_o + \frac{1}{h} RFRx_o - RFx_o)] =$$

$$= (I + FS_h + \frac{1}{h} RFS_h)Ry - \frac{1}{h}[Rx_o - hx_o - Rx_o] =$$

$$= (I + FS_h + \frac{1}{h} RFS_h)Ry + x_o.$$

An immediate consequence of this theorem is

Corollary 6.1. Suppose that all assumptions of Theorem 6.1 are satisfied. Then all S_h-periodic solutions of Equation (6.1) are of the form

$$x = (I + FS_h + \frac{1}{h} RFS_h)Ry + z, \quad \text{where } z \in Z_D \text{ is arbitrary.}$$

Corollary 6.2. Suppose that all assumptions of Theorem 6.1 are satisfied. Then for an arbitrary positive integer n the equation

$$D^nx = y, \quad y \in X_{S_h,1} \tag{6.3}$$

with the initial conditions

$$FD^kx = x_k, \quad x_k \in Z_D \quad (k = 0,1,\ldots,n-1) \tag{6.4}$$

has a unique S_h-periodic solution which is of the form:

$$x = [(I + FS_h + \frac{1}{h} RFS_h)R]^n y + \sum_{k=0}^{n-1} [(I + FS_h + \frac{1}{h} RFS_h)R]^k x_k. \quad (6.5)$$

Proof, by induction. For n = 1 our statement is just Theorem 6.1. Suppose that for an arbitrary fixed n the equation (6.3) together with the condition (6.4) has a unique S_h-periodic solution which is of the form (6.5). Write, as before, $R_1^o = (I + FS_h + (1/h) RFS_h)R$ and consider the equation

$$D^{n+1}x = y \ , \quad y \in X_{S_h,1} \quad (6.6)$$

with the initial conditions

$$FS^k x = x_k, \quad x_k \in Z_D \quad (k = 0,1,\ldots,n-1). \quad (6.7)$$

Write: $u = D^n x$ and consider the problem

$$Du = y, \quad Fu = x_n \ . \quad (6.8)$$

Theorem 6.1 implies that the problem (6.8) has a unique S_h-periodic solution which is of the form:

$$u = R_1^o y + x_n \ . \quad (6.9)$$

Now consider the problem

$$D^n x = u, \quad FD^k x = x_k \quad (k = 0,1,\ldots,n-1).$$

By our inductive assumption this problem has a unique S_h-periodic solution which is of the form

$$x = (R_1^o)^n u + \sum_{k=0}^{n-1} (R_1^o)^k x_k .$$

This and Formula (6.9) together imply that the unique S_h-periodic solution of the problem (6.6)-(6.7) we are looking for is of the form:

$$x = (R_1^o)^n u + \sum_{k=0}^{n-1} (R_1^o)^k x_k = (R_o^1)^n (R_o^1 y + x_n) + \sum_{k=0}^{n-1} (R_1^o)^k x_k =$$

$$= (R_1^o)^{n+1} y + \sum_{k=0}^{n} (R_1^o)^k x_k =$$

$$= [(I + FS_h + \frac{1}{h} RFS_h)R]^{n+1} y + \sum_{k=0}^{n} [(I + FS_h + \frac{1}{h} RFS_h)R]^k x_k ,$$

which was to be proved.

Corollary 6.3. Suppose that all assumptions of Theorem 6.1 are satisfied. Then for an arbitrary positive integer n all S_h-periodic solutions of Equation (6.3) are of the form

$$x = [(I + FS_h + \frac{1}{h} RFS_h)R]^n y + \sum_{k=0}^{n-1} [(I + FS_h + \frac{1}{h} RFS_h)r]^k z_k , \tag{6.10}$$

where $z_k \in Z_D$ are arbitrary $(k = 0,1,\dots,n-1)$.

Theorem 6.2. Suppose that all assumptions of Theorem 6.1 are satisfied. Suppose, moreover, that $\tilde{D} \in R(X)$, $\dim Z_{\tilde{D}} \neq 0$, $\tilde{F}$ is an initial operator for $\tilde{D}$ corresponding to an $\tilde{R} \in \mathscr{R}_{\tilde{D}}$ and $\tilde{S}_{\tilde{h}} \in L_0(X)$ is a $\tilde{D}$-invariant $\tilde{R}$-shift.

Write:

$$\tilde{R}_1^o = (I + \tilde{F}\tilde{S}_h + \frac{1}{\tilde{h}} \tilde{R}\tilde{F}\tilde{S}_{\tilde{h}})\tilde{R} . \tag{6.11}$$

If $y \in \tilde{X}_{\tilde{S}_h,1}$, $\tilde{R}_1^o y \in X_{S_h,1}$ then the equation

$$\tilde{D}Dx = y \tag{6.12}$$

together with the initial conditions

$$Fx = x_0, \ \tilde{F}Dx = \tilde{x}_0, \quad \text{where} \quad x_0 \in Z_D, \ \tilde{x}_0 \in Z_{\tilde{D}} \cap X_h \tag{6.13}$$

has a unique S_h-periodic solution

$$x = R_1^o\tilde{R}_1^o y + R_1^o\tilde{x}_0 + x_0 . \tag{6.14}$$

Proof: Since $\tilde{x}_0 \in Z_{\tilde{D}} \cap X_{S_h,1}$, we have $D\tilde{x}_0 = 0$ and $Sh\tilde{x}_0 = \tilde{x}_0$. Write: $u = Dx$. Theorem 6.1 implies that the equation $\tilde{D}u = y$ with the condition $\tilde{F}u = \tilde{x}_0$ has a unique $\tilde{S}_{\tilde{h}}$-periodic solution $u = \tilde{R}_1^o y + \tilde{x}_0$. Since $Dx = u$, we have an initial value problem:

$$Dx = \tilde{R}_1^o y + \tilde{x}_0 \ , \quad Fx = x_0 \ ,$$

where, by our assumptions, $\tilde{R}_1^o y + \tilde{x}_0 \in X_{S_h,1}$. Thus the last problem has a unique S_h-periodic solution

$$x = R_1^o(\tilde{R}_1^o y + \tilde{x}_o) + x_o = \tilde{R}_1^o R_1 y + R_1^o \tilde{x}_o + x_o .$$

An immediate consequence is

Corollary 6.4. Suppose that all assumptions of Theorem 6.2 are satisfied. If $y \in \tilde{X}_{\tilde{S}_h,1}$, $\tilde{R}_1^o y \in X_{S_h,1}$ then all S_h-periodic solutions of Equation (6.12) are of the form

$$x = R_1^o \tilde{R}_1^o y + R_1^o z_1 + z_o, \quad \text{where } z_o \in Z_D,\ z_1 \in Z_{\tilde{D}} \cap X_h, \tag{6.15}$$

are arbitrary.

Corollary 6.5. Suppose that all assumptions of Theorem 6.2 are satisfied. Suppose, moreover, that D and $\tilde{D}$ are commutative and

$$y,\ R_1^o y,\ \tilde{R}_1^o y \in X_{S_h,1} \cap X_{\tilde{S}_{\tilde{h}},1} .$$

Then Equation (6.12) has solutions of the form (6.15) which are S_h-periodic and $\tilde{S}_{\tilde{h}}$-periodic simultaneously.

It is an immediate consequence of Corollary 6.3, if we apply the equality $D\tilde{D} = \tilde{D}D$ on $\mathscr{D}_{D\cap\tilde{D}}$ and change the role of D and $\tilde{D}$ in the proof of Theorem 6.2.

Proposition 6.1. Suppose that $D \in R(X)$, $\dim Z_D \neq 0$, F is an initial operator for D corresponding to an $R \in \mathscr{R}_D$, $S_h \in L_o(X)$ is a D-invariant R-shift on $h \neq 0$ and D_1 is defined by Formula (3.13). Then

$$D_1^n F = (-1)^n h^n F \quad \text{on } X_{S_h,1} \quad (n = 0,1,2,\ldots) \tag{6.16}$$

Proof, by induction. For n = 0 Formula (6.16) becomes trivial. For n = 1, since DF = 0 and $F^2 = F, FS_h = F$ on $X_{S_h,1}$ we have by definition: $D_1F = (D - (1/h)F)F = -(1/h)F^2 = -h^{-1}F$. Suppose Formula (6.16) to be true for an arbitrary positive integer $n \geq 1$. Then $D_1^{n+1}F = D_1(D_1^nF) = D_1(-h)^{-n}F = (-h)^{-n}D_1F = = (-h)^{-n}(-h)^{-1}F = (-h)^{n+1}F$, which was to be proved.

Proposition 6.2. Suppose that all assumptions of Proposition 6.1 are satisfied. Then

$$D^n = D_1^n + F_n^h \quad \text{on} \quad X_{S_h,1}^{(n)} = X_{S_h,1} \cap \mathscr{D}_{D^n} \quad (n = 0,1,2,\ldots), \tag{6.17}$$

where

$$F_n^h = \sum_{j=0}^{n-1} (-1)^{n-1-j} h^{-n+j} FD^j \quad (n = 1,2,\ldots), \quad F_o^h = 0. \tag{6.18}$$

Proof, by induction. For n = 0 Formula (6.17) becomes trivial. For n = 1 the definition of D_1 implies that on $X_{S_h,1}$ we have $D = D_1 + (1/h)FS_h = D_1 + (1/h)F = D_1 + F_1^h$. Suppose Formula (6.17) to be true for an arbitrary positive integer n. Proposition 6.1 implies that on $X_{S_h,1}^{(n+1)}$ we have

$$D^{n+1} = D^nD = (D_1^n + F_n^h)D = D_1^n(D_1 + \frac{1}{h} F) + \sum_{j=0}^{n-1} (-1)^{n-1-j} h^{-n+j} FD^j D =$$

$$= D_1^{n+1} + h^{-1}D_1^nF + \sum_{j=0}^{n-1} (-1)^{n-1-j} h^{-n+j} FD^{j+1} =$$

$$= D_1^{n+1} + h^{-1}(-h)^{-n}F + \sum_{m=1}^{n} (-1)^{n-m} h^{-n+m-1} FD^m =$$

$$= D_1^{n+1} + (-1)^n h^{-(n+1)} F + \sum_{m=1}^{n} (-1)^{n-m} h^{-(n+1)+m} FD^m =$$

$$= D_1^{n+1} + \sum_{m=0}^{n} (-1)^{n-m} h^{-(n+1)+m} FD^m = D_1^{n+1} + F_{n+1}^h ,$$

which was to be proved.

An immediate consequence of Proposition 6.2 is

<u>Corollary 6.6.</u> Suppose that all assumptions of Proposition 6.1 are satisfied. Then

$$D^n x = D_1^n x + \hat{x}_n \quad \text{for all} \quad x \in X_{S_h,1}^{(n)} = X_{S_h,1} \cap \mathscr{D}_{D^n}, \tag{6.19}$$

where

$$\hat{x}_n = \sum_{j=0}^{n-1} (-1)^{n-1-j} h^{-n+j} FD^j x \in Z_D \; (n = 1,2,\ldots), \; \hat{x}_o = 0. \tag{6.20}$$

<u>Theorem 6.3.</u> Suppose that $D \in R(X)$, $\dim Z_D \neq 0$, F is an initial operator for D corresponding to an $R \in \mathscr{R}_D$, $S_h \in L_o(X)$ is a D-invariant R-shift on $h \neq 0$ and D_1, F_1, R_1^o are defined by Formulae (3.13), (3.20). Write, as before

$$Q(D) = \sum_{k=0}^{N} Q_k D^k, \text{ where } Q_k \in L_o(X),\; S_h Q_k = Q_k S_h \tag{6.21}$$

$$(k = 0,1,\ldots,N-1),\; Q_N = I$$

$$Q(t,S) = \sum_{k=0}^{N} Q_k t^k S^{N-k} . \tag{6.22}$$

If the operator $Q(I,R_1^o)$ is invertible in the space $X_{S_h,1}^{(N)}$ then the equation

$$Q(D)x = y, \quad y \in X_{S_h,1} \tag{6.23}$$

together with the initial conditions

$$FD^k x = x_k, \; x_k \in Z_D \quad (k = 0,1,2,\ldots,N-1) \tag{6.24}$$

has a unique S_h-periodic solution

$$x = (R_1^o)^N [Q(I,R_1^o)]^{-1} (y - y_o), \tag{6.25}$$

where

$$y_o = \sum_{k=1}^{N} Q_k \sum_{j=0}^{k-1} (-1)^{k-1-j} h^{-k+1} x_j \in X_{S_h,1} . \tag{6.26}$$

Proof: Observe that coefficients Q_k, as S_h-periodic operators, preserve the space $X_{S_h,1}$. Corollary 6.6 implies that

$$y = Q(D)x = \sum_{k=0}^{N} Q_k D^k x = \sum_{k=0}^{N} Q_k (D_1^k x + \hat{x}_k) =$$

$$= \sum_{k=0}^{N} Q_k D_1^k + \sum_{k=1}^{N} Q_k \sum_{j=0}^{k-1} (-1)^{k-1-j} h^{-k+j} FD^j x =$$

$$= Q(D_1) + \sum_{k=1}^{N} Q_k \sum_{j=0}^{k-1} (-1)^{k-1-j} h^{-k+j} x_j = Q(D_1)x + y_o,$$

because $\hat{x}_o = 0$. Observe that $y_o \in X_{S_h,1}$. Indeed, since all constants $x_j \in X_{S_h,1}$ and operators Q_k are S_h-periodic, we find

$$S_h y_0 = \sum_{k=1}^{N} S_h Q_k \sum_{j=0}^{k-1} (-1)^{k-1-j} h^{-k+j} x_j =$$

$$= \sum_{k=1}^{N} Q_k \sum_{j=0}^{k-1} (-1)^{k-1-j} h^{-k+j} S_h x_j =$$

$$= \sum_{k=1}^{N} Q_k \sum_{j=0}^{k-1} (-1)^{k-1-j} h^{-k+j} x_j = y_0 .$$

We have obtained the equation

$$Q(D_1)x = y - y_0, \quad \text{where } y - y_0 \in X_{S_h,1}. \tag{6.27}$$

Put $u = D_1^N x$. Then $x = (R_1^o)^N u$ because $D_1 R_1^o = R_1^o D_1 = I$ on $X_{S_h,1}$. Hence

$$y - y_0 = Q(D_1)x = Q(D_1)(R_1^o)^N u = \sum_{k=0}^{N} Q_k D_1^k (R_1^o)^N_u =$$

$$= \sum_{k=0}^{N} Q_k (R_1^o)^{N-k} u = Q(I,R_1^o)u.$$

But the operator $Q(I,R_1^o)$ is invertible in the space $X_{S_h,1}$, which implies that $u = [Q(I,R_1^o)]^{-1}(y-y_0)$ and $x = (R_1^o)^N u = (R_1^o)^N [Q(I,R_1^o)]^{-1}(y-y_0)$. This is the unique S_h-periodic solution of the problem (6.23), (6.24) that we were looking for.

An immediate consequence of Theorem 6.3 and Corollary 6.6 is

Corollary 6.7. Suppose that all assumptions of Theorem 6.3 are satisfied and that the operator $Q(I,R_1^o)$ is invertible. Then all S_h-periodic solutions of Equation (6.23) are of the form

$$x = (R_1^o)^N [Q(I,R_1^o)]^{-1}(y - \sum_{k=1}^{N} Q_k z_k) , \tag{6.28}$$

where $z_1,\dots,z_N \in Z_D$ are arbitrary.

Corollary 6.8. Suppose that all assumptions of Theorem 6.3 are satisfied and that the operator $Q(I,R_1^o)$ is invertible. Then all S_h-periodic solutions of the equation

$$D^M Q(D)x = y,\ y \in X_{S_h,1} \quad (M \geqslant 0) \tag{6.29}$$

are of the form

$$x = (R_1^o)^N [Q(I,R_1^o)]^{-1}[(R_1^o)^M y + \sum_{k=0}^{M-1} (R_1^o)^k z_{N+k+1} - \sum_{k=1}^{N} Q_k z_k], \tag{6.30}$$

where $z_1,\dots,z_{N+M} \in Z_D$ are arbitrary.

Proof: Put $u = Q(D)x$. Then we have the equation $D^M u = y$. Corollary 6.2 implies

$$u = (R_1^o)^M y + \sum_{k=0}^{n-1} (R_1^o)^k z_{N+k}, \quad \text{where } z_{N+K} \in Z_D \text{ are arbitrary.}$$

Having already determined u, we apply Corollary 6.7 and we obtain

$$x = (R_1^o)^N [Q(I,R_1^o)]^{-1}(u - \sum_{k=1}^{N} Q_k z_k) =$$

$$= (R_1^o)^N [Q(I,R_1^o)]^{-1}[(R_1^o)^M y + \sum_{k=0}^{M-1} (R_1^o)^k z_{N+k+1} - \sum_{k=1}^{N} Q_k z_k]$$

where $z_1,\dots,z_{N+M} \in Z_D$ are arbitrary.

Corollary 6.9. Suppose that all assumptions of Theorem 6.3

are satisfied and that the operator $Q(I,R_1^o)$ is invertible. Then all S_h-periodic solutions of the equation

$$Q(D)D^M x = y, \quad y \in X_{S_h,1} \quad (M \geq 0) \tag{6.31}$$

are of the form

$$x = (R_1^o)^{M+N}[Q(I,R_1^o)]^{-1}\,(y - \sum_{k=1}^{N} Q_k z_k) + \sum_{k=0}^{M-1} (R_1^o)^k z_{N+k+1}, \tag{6.32}$$

where $z_1,\ldots,z_{N+M} \in Z_D$ are arbitrary.

Proof: Put $u = D^M x$. Corollary 6.7 implies that all S_h-periodic solutions of the equation $Q(D)u = y$ are of the form

$$u = (R_1^o)^N[Q(I,R_1^o)]^{-1}(y - \sum_{k=1}^{N} Q_k z_k), \quad \text{where}$$

$z_1,\ldots,z_N$ are arbitrary.

Corollary 6.2 implies then that

$$x = (R_1^o)^M u + \sum_{k=0}^{M-1} (R_1^o)^k z_{N+k+1} =$$

$$= (R_1^o)^M\{(R_1^o)^N[Q(I,R_1^o)]^{-1}(y - \sum_{k=1}^{N} Q_k z_k)\} + \sum_{k=0}^{M-1} (R_1^o)^k z_{N+k+1} =$$

$$= (R_1^o)^{M+N}[Q(I,R_1^o)]^{-1}(y - \sum_{k=1}^{N} Q_k z_k) + \sum_{k=0}^{M-1} (R_1^o)^k z_{N+k+1},$$

where $z_1,\ldots,z_{N+M} \in Z_D$ are arbitrary.

Theorem 6.4. Suppose that $D \in R(X)$, $\dim Z_D \neq 0$, F is an initial operator for an $R \in \mathscr{R}_D$, $S_h \in L_o(X)$ is a D-invariant R-shift on $h \neq 0$ and D_1 is defined by Formulae (3.13). If for a scalar λ the operator $I + \lambda R$ is invertible in the space X then

1° the operator $I + \lambda R$ mapping the space

$$\hat{X}_{S_h,1} = \{x \in X_{S_h,1} : FS_hRx = 0\} \tag{6.33}$$

into $X^{(1)}_{S_h,1}$ has an inverse mapping $X^{(1)}_{S_h,1}$ into $\hat{X}_{S_h,1}$;*)

2° an initial value problem

$$(D + \lambda I)x = y, \quad y \in X_{S_h,1} \tag{6.34}$$

$$Fx = x_o, \quad x_o \in Z_D \tag{6.35}$$

has a unique S_h-periodic solution

$$x = (I + \lambda R)^{-1}(Ry - \frac{1}{h} Rx_o - x_o) \tag{6.36}$$

3° All S_h-periodic solutions of Equation (6.34) are of the form

$$x = (I + \lambda R)^{-1}(Ry - \frac{1}{h} Rz + z), \text{ where } z \in Z_D \text{ is arbitrary.} \tag{6.37}$$

---

*cf. Theorem 3.3 and Example 3.2

Proof: Observe that for all $x \in \hat{X}_{S_h,1}$ we have $R_1^o =$ $(I + FS_h + 1/h\ RFS_h)Rx + FS_hRx + (1/h)RFS_hRx = Rx$. This, our assumption that the operator $I + \lambda R$ has an inverse in X, and Theorem 3.3 together imply that the operator $I + \lambda R$ has an inverse mapping $X_{S_h,1}^{(1)}$ into $\hat{X}_{S_h,1}$. Consider now the problem (6.34)-(6.35). Since for all $x \in X_{S_h,1}^{(1)} = X_{S_h,1} \cap \mathscr{D}_D$ we have $D_1x = Dx - (1/h)FS_hx$ $= Dx - (1/h)Fx = Dx - (1/h)x_o$ and $D_1R = D_1R_1^o = I$ on $X_{S_h,1}^{(1)}$, we can rewrite Equation (6.34) as follows:

$$D_1(I + \lambda R)x = y - \frac{1}{h}x_o .$$

Theorem 3.3 implies that $RD_1 = I - F$ on $X_{S_h,1}$. Then $(I + \lambda R)x =$ $= R(y - (1/h)x_o) + Fx = R(y - (1/h)x_o) + x_o$ and $x = (I + \lambda R)^{-1}$ $(Ry - (1/h)Rx_o + x_o)$ is the unique S_h-periodic solution, we were looking for. An immediate consequence of this fact is that all S_h-periodic solutions of Equation 6.34 are of the form (6.37).

<u>Corollary 6.10.</u> Suppose that all assumptions of Theorem 6.4 are satisfied. Write:

$$Q(D) = \sum_{k=0}^{N} q_kD^k, \quad \text{where } q_o,\ldots,q_{N-1} \in \mathbb{C}, \quad {}_N = 1 \qquad (6.38)$$

$$Q(t,s) = \sum_{k=0}^{N} q_kt^ks^{N-k} . \qquad (6.39)$$

Suppose then $R \in V(X)$. Then

1° The operator $Q(I,R)$ has an inverse mapping $X_{S_h,1}^{(n)}$ into $\hat{X}_{S_h,1}$;

2° All S_h-periodic solutions of the equation

$$D^M Q(D)x = Q(D)D^M x = y \ , \quad y \in X_{S_h,1} \quad (M \geq 0) \tag{6.40}$$

are of the form

$$x = R^{M+N}[Q(I,R)]^{-1}(y - \sum_{k=1}^{N} q_k z_k) + \sum_{k=0}^{M-1} R^k z_{N+k+1} \tag{6.41}$$

where $z_1,\ldots,z_{N+M} \in Z_D$ are arbitrary.

Proof: We can write: $Q(t) = \Pi_{j=1}^{n} (t-t_j)^{r_j}$, $t_j \neq t_k$ for $j \neq k$, $r_1 + \ldots + r_n = N$. Since R is a Volterra operator, the operator $Q(I,R) = \Sigma_{j=1}^{n}(I-t_jR)^{r_j}$ is invertible as a superposition of invertible operators. This, Theorem 6.4 and Corollary 6.9 together imply the conclusions of our theorem.

7 Perturbations theorems

We shall now consider equations with shifts. Without loss of generality we can consider equations of order 1, because we have seen that equations of a higher order could be studied in a similar way as in the preceding section under appropriate assumptions. We have

Theorem 7.1. Suppose that $D \in R(X)$, $\dim Z_D \neq 0$, F is an initial operator for D corresponding to an $R \in \mathscr{R}_D$, S_h is an R-shift (on $0 \neq h \in A(\mathbb{R})$). Write:

$$A(S) = \sum_{k=0}^{n-1} A_k S_h^k \ , \quad \text{where} \quad A_k S_h = S_h A_k \quad \text{for } k = 0,1,\ldots,n-1. \tag{7.1}$$

Then a unique S_h^n-periodic solution of the equation

$$Dx = A(S_h)x + y, \quad y \in X_{S_h,n} \tag{7.2}$$

satisfying the initial condition

$$Fx = x_o, \quad x_o \in Z_D \tag{7.3}$$

is of the form

$$x = [I - R_n^o A(S)]^{-1} R_n^o (y - \frac{1}{nh} x_o) \ , \tag{7.4}$$

provided that the operator $I - R_n^o A(S)$ is invertible, where

$$R_n^o = (I + FS_{nh} RFS_{nh})R \ . \tag{7.5}$$

Proof: Our assumptions and Theorem 3.1 together imply that $S_{nh}x = S_h^n x = x$ and $FS_{nh}x = Fx = x_o$, the operator $R_n^o = (I + FS_{nh} + (1/nh)RFS_{nh})R$ is invertible on the space $X_{S_h,n}$ and

$$x = R_n^o D_n x = R_n^o (D - \frac{1}{nh} FS_{nh})x = R_n^o (Dx - \frac{1}{nh} Fx) =$$

$$= R_n^o [A(S)x + y - \frac{1}{nh} x_o],$$

i.e.

$$[I - R_n^o A(S)]x = R_n^o (y - \frac{1}{nh} x_o) \ .$$

Since the operator $I - R_n^o A(S)$ is invertible by our assumptions, we conclude that x is of the required form.

Corollary 7.1. Suppose that all assumptions of Theorem 7.1 are satisfied and the operator $I - R_n^o A(S)$ is invertible. Then all S_{nh}-periodic solutions of Equation (7.1) are of the form

$$x = [I - R_n^o A(S)]^{-1} R_n^o (y - \frac{1}{nh} z), \quad \text{where } z \in Z_D \text{ is arbitrary.} \tag{7.6}$$

Theorem 7.2. Suppose that X is a Banach space, $D \in R(X)$ $\dim Z_D \neq 0$, F is a bounded initial operator for D corresponding to a compact $R \in \mathscr{R}_D \cap V(X)$, $\{S_h\}_{h \in A(\mathbb{R})}$ are bounded D-shifts. Suppose, moreover, that the set $E(R)$ of exponential elements is dense in X. Write:

$$R_n^o = (I + FS_{nh} + \frac{1}{nh} RFS_{nh})R , \tag{7.8}$$

$$\tilde{R}_n^o = (I + FS_{nh'} + \frac{1}{nh} RFS_{nh'})R, \quad h \neq h' \in A(\mathbb{R}). \tag{7.9}$$

Then

$$\lim_{h' \to h} \| (S_{h'} - S_h)x \| = 0 \quad \text{for all} \quad x \in X \quad h \in A(\mathbb{R}), \tag{7.10}$$

$$\lim_{h' \to h} \| (\tilde{R}_n^o - R_n^o)x \| = 0, \quad \text{for all} \quad x \in X, \quad n \in \mathbb{N}, h \in A(\mathbb{R}). \tag{7.11}$$

Proof: Since $\{S_h\}_{h \in A(\mathbb{R})}$ are D-shifts and the multiplication of elements by scalars is continuous, we find for all $e_\lambda(z)$, where $\lambda \in \mathbb{C}$, $z \in Z_D$ are arbitrary:

$$(S_{h'} - S_h)e_\lambda(z) = (e^{-\lambda h'} - e^{-\lambda h})e_\lambda(z) =$$

$$= e^{-\lambda h'}[1 - e^{-\lambda(h-h')}]e_\lambda(z) \to 0 \quad \text{as} \quad h' \to h.$$

Since the set $E(R)$ is dense in X, we conclude that

$$\| (S_{h'} - S_h)s \| \to 0 \quad \text{as} \quad h' \to h \text{ for all } x \in X.$$

An immediate consequence of Formula (7.10) is that

$$\lim_{h'\to h} \| (S_{nh'} - S_{nh})x \| = 0 \quad \text{for all} \quad x \in X \ (n \in \mathbb{N},\ h \in A(\mathbb{R})). \tag{7.12}$$

This, and our assumptions together imply for all $x \in X$ that we have (since $Rx \in X$)

$$\| (\tilde{R}_n^o - R_n^o)x \| = \| [(I + FS_{nh} + \frac{1}{nh} RFS_{nh}) - (I + FS_{nh'} + \frac{1}{nh} RFS_{nh'})]Rx \|$$

$$= \| [F(S_{nh} - S_{nh'}) + \frac{1}{nh} RF(S_{nh} - S_{nh'})]Rx \| \leqslant$$

$$\leqslant \| F \| \, \| (S_{nh} - S_{nh'})Rx \| + \frac{1}{n|h|} \| R \| \cdot \| F \| \cdot \| (S_{nh} - S_{nh'})Rx \| \leqslant$$

$$\leqslant [\| F \| \, (1 + \frac{1}{n|h|} \| R \|)] \, \| (S_{nh} - S_{nh'})Rx \| \to 0$$

as $h' \to h$.

<u>Theorem 7.3.</u> Suppose that X is a Banach space, $D \in R(X)$, $\dim Z_D \neq 0$, F is a bounded initial operator for D corresponding to a compact $R \in \mathscr{R}_D$, $\{S_h\}_{h\in A(\mathbb{R})}$ are bounded R-shifts. Suppose, moreover that the set $P(R)$ of D-polynomials is dense in X and that R_n^o and $\tilde{R}_n^o$ are defined by Formulae (7.8), (7.9). Then Formulae (7.10) and (7.11) hold.

Proof: Since $\{S_h\}_{h\in A(\mathbb{R})}$ are R-shifts and the multiplication of elements by scalars is continuous, we find for all $z \in Z_D$, $k \in \mathbb{N} \cup \{0\}$:

$$(S_{h'} - S_h)R^k z = \sum_{j=0}^{k} \frac{(-1)^{k-j}}{(k-j)!} (h'^{k-j} - h^{k-j})R^k z =$$

$$= (h'-h) \sum_{j=0}^{k} \frac{(-1)^{k-j}}{(k-j)!} \left(\sum_{m=0}^{k-j-1} h'^m h^{k-j-m} \right) R^k z \to 0$$

as $h' \to h$.

Since the set $P(R)$ is dense in X we conclude that

$$\| (S_{h'} - S_h)x \| \to 0 \quad \text{as} \quad h' \to h \quad \text{for all} \quad x \in X.$$

The remainder of the proof goes along the same lines as the proof of Theorem 7.2.

Corollary 7.1. Suppose that either the assumptions of Theorem 7.2 or the assumptions of Theorem 7.3 are satisfied. Write:

$$A(t) = \sum_{k=0}^{n-1} A_k t^k, \quad \text{where } A_k \text{ are bounded and}$$

$$S_k A_k = A_k S_h \; (k = 0,1,\dots,n-1); \tag{7.13}$$

$$B_h = R_n^o A(S_h), \quad B_{h'} = \tilde{R}_n^o A(S_{h'}) . \tag{7.14}$$

Then

$$\lim_{h'\to h} \| (B_{h'} - B_h)x \| = 0 \quad \text{for all} \quad x \in X \; (h \in A(\mathbb{R})). \tag{7.15}$$

Proof: We have for all $x \in X$

$$\| (B_{h'} - B_h)x \| = \| [R_h^o A(S_h) R_h^o A(S_h)]x \| \leqslant$$

$$\leq \| R_n^o[A(S_{h'}) - A(S_h)]x\| + \|(\tilde{R}_h^o - R_h^o)A(S_h)x\| .$$

Write:

$$b = (a + \|F\| \cdot \|S_{nh'}\| + \frac{1}{n|h|}\|R\| \cdot \|F\| \|S_{nh'}\|)\|R\| . \quad (7.16)$$

Since $S_{h'}$ and S_h are either D-shifts or R-shifts we have for all $k \in \mathbb{N}$

$$S_n^k - S_{kh} , S_{h'}^k = S_{kh'}$$

(Theorem 5.5 and 5.7). This, and Formulae (7.10), (7.11) together imply that for all $x \in X$ we have, if we write $\tilde{x} = A(S_h)x \in X$,

$$\|(B_{h'} - B_h)x\| \leq b\|[A(S_{h'}) - A(S_h)]x\| + \|(\tilde{R}_n^o - R_n^o)\tilde{x}\| =$$

$$= b\|\sum_{k=0}^{n-1} A_k(S_{h'}^k - S_h^k)x\| + \|(\tilde{R}_n^o - R_n^o)\tilde{x}\| \leq$$

$$\leq b \sum_{k=0}^{n-1} \|A_k\| \|S_{kh'} - S_{nh})x\| + \|(\tilde{R}_n^o - R_n^o)\tilde{x}\| \to 0$$

as $h' \to h$.

<u>Theorem 7.4.</u> Suppose that all assumptions of Theorem 7.1 are satisfied. Let operators $A(t)$, B_h, $B_{h'}$ be defined by Formulae (7.13) and (7.14). Consider the equation

$$Dx = A(S_h)x + y, \quad y \in X_{S_h,n} , \quad (7.17)$$

and a perturbed equation

$$D\tilde{x} = A(S_{h'})\tilde{x} + y, \ y \in X_{S_h,n} \ . \tag{7.18}$$

If the operator $B_h = I - R_n^o A(S)$ is invertible then Equation (7.17) with the condition $Fx = x_o$ has a unique S_{nh}-periodic solution

$$x = [I - R_n^o A(S_h)]^{-1} R_n^o (y - \frac{1}{nh} x_o) \ . \tag{7.19}$$

Moreover, there exists a $\delta > 0$ such that for $|h'-h| < \delta$ the operator $B_{h'}$ is invertible, and the perturbed equation (7.18) with the condition $Fx = x_o$ also has a unique S_{nh}-periodic solution $\tilde{x}$ of the form

$$\tilde{x} = [I - R_n^o A(S_{h'})]^{-1} \tilde{R}_n^o (y - \frac{1}{nh} x_o) \tag{7.20}$$

such that $\lim_{h' \to h} \| \tilde{x} - x \| = 0$.

Proof: If the operator $B_h = I - R_n^o A(S)$ is invertible then Theorem 6.3 implies that Equation (7.17) together with the condition $Fx = x_o$ has a unique S_{nh}-periodic solution which is of the form (7.19). Rewrite Equation (7.17) in the form

$$[I - R_n^o A(S_h)]x = R_n^o (y - \frac{1}{nh} x_o), \tag{7.21}$$

or more simply:

$$(I - B_h)x = R_n^o y_h, \quad \text{where} \quad y_h = y - \frac{1}{nh} x_o \ . \tag{7.22}$$

The perturbed equation (7.18) together with the condition $Fx = x_0$ can be rewritten as follows:

$$[I - \tilde{R}_n^o A(S_{h'})]\tilde{x} = \tilde{R}_n^o(y - \frac{1}{nh} x_0) \tag{7.23}$$

or more simply:

$$(I - B_{h'})x = \tilde{R}_n^o y_h . \tag{7.24}$$

Since R is compact by our assumption, we conclude that the operator $R_n^o = (I + FS_{nh} + (1/nh)RFS_h)R$ is compact. Then the operator $B_h = R_n^o A(S)$ is also compact. The operator $I - B_h = I - R_n^o A(S)$ is invertible by our assumption. We have

$$I - B_{h'} = I - B_h + B_h - B_{h'} = (I - B_h)[I + (I - B_h)^{-1}(B_h - B_{h'})]$$

i.e.

$$I - B_{h'} = (I - B_h)(I - T), \quad \text{where} \quad T = (I - B_h)^{-1}(B_{h'} - B_h). \tag{7.25}$$

Corollary 7.1 implies that there exists a $\delta > 0$ such that $\|Tx\| < q < 1$ for all $x \in X$. Thus the operator $I - B_{h'}$ is an invertible operator. Rewrite Equation (7.24) applying Equality (7.25):

$$(I - T)\tilde{x} = (I - B_h)^{-1}\tilde{R}_n^o y_h . \tag{7.26}$$

Since the norm of $T\tilde{x}$ is less than 1, the Neumann theorem implies that Equation (7.18) has a unique solution

$$\tilde{x} = (I-T)^{-1}(I-B_h)^{-1}\tilde{R}^o_n y_n . \tag{7.27}$$

But $(I-B_h)^{-1}R^o_n y_n = x$, and thus we have

$$(I-T)\tilde{x} = (I-B_h)^{-1}\tilde{R}^o_n y_n = (I-B_n)^{-1}(\tilde{R}^o_n - R^o_n)y_h + (I-B_h)^{-1}R^o_n y_h =$$

$$= (I-B_h)^{-1}(\tilde{R}^o_n - R^o_n)y_h + x.$$

Since $T = (I-B_h)^{-1}(B_{h'}-B_h)$, Theorem 7.1 and Corollary 7.1 together imply that

$$\|\tilde{x}-x\| = \|(I-B_h)^{-1}(\tilde{R}^o_n - R^o_n)y_h\| + \|Tx\| \leqslant$$

$$\leqslant \|(I-B_h)^{-1}\|[\|(\tilde{R}^o_n - R^o_n)y_h\| + \|(B_{h'}-B_h)x\| \to 0$$

$$\text{as } h' \to h.$$

We therefore conclude that the perturbed equation together with the condition $Fx = x_o$ has a unique S_{nh}-periodic solution for $|h'-h|$ sufficiently small.

This theorem generalizes theorems on small perturbations of deviations preserving periodic solutions of linear differential-difference equations with periodic coefficients. (cf. the author and S. Rolewicz [1], S. Rolewicz [1]).

We shall consider now a non-linear periodic problem.

Theorem 7.4. Suppose that:

1° $D \in R(X)$, $\dim Z_D \neq 0$, F is a bounded initial operator for D corresponding to an $R \in \mathcal{R}_D$;

2° $\{S_h\}_{h\in A(\mathbb{R})}$ are either D-shifts (provided that $R \in V(X)$) or R-shifts and the semigroup (group) $\{S_h\}_{h\in A(\mathbb{R})}$ is strongly continuous, moreover, D is its infinitesimal generator;

3° G is a non-linear mapping of X into $X \times \mathbb{R}$ such that the functions $\hat{G}(h,\hat{x}(h)\mu)$, $\partial G/\partial\hat{x}\ (h,\hat{x}(h),\mu)$ are continuous in both variables and ω-periodic with respect to the variables h, where $\hat{x},\hat{G}$ are defined by the canonical mapping (5.1):

$$\hat{x}(h) = FS_h,\ \hat{G}(h,\hat{x}(h),\mu) = FS_hG(x,\mu) \qquad \text{for all}\ \ x \in X,\ \mu \in \mathbb{R},\ h \in A(\mathbb{R}). \tag{7.28}$$

If the linearized equation

$$\frac{d\hat{y}(h)}{dh} = \frac{\partial}{\partial\hat{y}}\hat{G}(h,\hat{y}(h),\mu)\Big|_{(h,\hat{y}(h),0)} \tag{7.29}$$

has a unique ω-periodic solution $\hat{y} = 0$, then the equation

$$Dx = G(x,\mu) \tag{7.30}$$

for sufficiently small $|\mu|$ has an S_ω-periodic solution $x(\mu)$ such that

$$\hat{x}(h,0) = \hat{y}(h) \quad \text{for all}\ \ h \in A(\mathbb{R}) \quad \text{and} \quad \hat{x}(h,\mu) \tag{7.31}$$

is continuous with respect to (h,μ).

Proof: Theorems 5.3, 5.5 (or 5.7) together imply that, by our assumptions 1° and 2°, we have

$$\frac{d}{dh}\hat{x}(h) = Dx \quad \text{for all} \quad x \in \mathscr{D}_D$$

Thus, instead of Equation (7.30) we can consider the equation

$$\hat{x}'(h) = G(h,\hat{x}(h),\mu), \tag{7.32}$$

where $\hat{G}(h,\hat{x}(h),\mu)$ is defined by Formulae (7.28). It is well-known (cf. Coddington and Levinson [1], Chapter XIV, §1) that under assumptions 3°, if the linearized equation has a unique ω-periodic solution $y(h) \equiv 0$ then Equation (7.32) has for sufficiently small $|\omega|$ an ω-periodic solution $\hat{x}(h,\mu)$ such that Equality (7.31) holds and $\hat{x}(h,\mu)$ is continuous with respect to (h,μ). But this means that there exists an $x \in X$ which is S_ω-periodic and such that $\hat{x}(h,0) = \hat{y}(h)$, where $\hat{x}(h) = FS_hx$, $h \in A(\mathbb{R})$. Indeed, for all $h \in A(\mathbb{R})$ we have $\hat{x}(h+\omega) = FS_{h+\omega}x = FS_hS_\omega x = FS_hx$, for $S_\omega x = x$.

8 Exponential - periodic elements

Suppose that X is a commutative linear ring over a field $\mathscr{F}$, (where either $\mathscr{F} = \mathbb{C}$ or $\mathscr{F} = \mathbb{R}$) $D \in R(X)$, $\dim Z_D \neq 0$ and that there exists an $R \in \mathscr{R}_D \cap V(X)$.

We shall consider *exponential-periodic elements* i.e. elements of the form

$$x = e_\lambda(z)v, \quad \text{where} \quad z \in Z_D, \ \lambda \in \quad , \ v \in \mathscr{D}_D \ , \ Sv = v, \tag{8.1}$$

where $S \in L_o(X)$ is a D-invariant operator, and linear combina= tons of such elements.

We recall (cf. the author [10]) that a commutative linear ring X is called:

(a) a quasi-Leibniz ring (briefly: *QL-ring*) if for a $D \in R(X)$ there exists a scalar d such that

$$D(xy) = xDy + yDx + d(Dx)(Dy) \quad \text{for all} \quad x,y \in \mathscr{D}_D \ , \tag{8.2}$$

(b) a Leibniz ring (briefly: *L-ring*) if X is a QL-ring with $d = 0$, i.e. if for a $D \in R(X)$ we have

$$D(xy) = xDy + yDx \quad \text{for all} \quad x,y \in \mathscr{D}_D \ . \tag{8.3}$$

(c) a Duhamel ring (briefly: *Dh-ring*) if for a $D \in R(X)$ there exist linear functionals f_1, f_2, g_1, g_2 defined on X such that

$$D(xy) = xDy + f_1(x)Dy + f_2(y)Dx + g_1(x)y + g_2(y)x \tag{8.4}$$

for all $x, y \in \mathscr{D}_D$.

If $f_1 = g_1 = f_2 = g_2 = 0$ in a Dh-ring, i.e. if

$$D(xy) = xDy \quad \text{for} \quad x, y \in \mathscr{D}_D \tag{8.4'}$$

then we shall say briefly that X is a *Dh_o-ring*.

We recall also that in a Dh_o-ring either $\dim Z_D = 0$ or X has divisors of zero, provided that there exists an $R \in \mathscr{R}_D \cap V(X)$ (cf. (cf. Proposition 5 of the author's paper [10]).

The following question arises: We have assumed that S is a D-invariant operator, i.e.

$$SD = DS \quad \text{on } \mathscr{D}_D. \tag{8.5}$$

Does Equality (8.5) hold for exponential-periodic elements of the form (8.1) in QL-rings, L-rings and Dh-rings?

The answer is given by the following

<u>Theorem 8.1.</u> Suppose that $D \in R(X)$, $\dim Z_D \neq 0$ and there is an $R \in \mathscr{R}_D \cap V(X)$. Suppose that an operator $S \in L_o(X)$ has the following property:

$$\underset{0\neq r\in\mathbb{R}}{\exists}\quad \underset{\lambda\in\mathbb{C}}{\forall}\quad \underset{z\in Z_D}{\forall}\quad Se_\lambda(z) = e^{\lambda r}e_\lambda(z)\ ^{*} \tag{8.6}$$

If X is either a QL-ring or a Dh_o-ring then Equality (8.5) holds on the set

$$X^o = \{x = e_\lambda(z)v : \lambda \in \mathbb{C},\ z \in Z_D,\ v \in \mathscr{D}_D,\ Sv = v\}\ . \tag{8.7}$$

(where we denote, as before, $e_\lambda = (I-\lambda R)^{-1}$).

Proof: Let $x = e_\lambda(z)v \in X^o$ be arbitrarily fixed. Write: $u = e_\lambda(z)$. Observe that by our assumption

$$SDv = DSv = Dv,\ Du = De_\lambda(z) = \lambda e_\lambda(z) = \lambda u. \tag{8.8}$$

Suppose that X is a QL-ring. Then our assumption that the operator S is multiplicative, Property (8.6) and Formulae (8.8) together imply that

$$DSx = DS(uv) = D[(Su)(Sv)] = (Su)(DSv) + (Sv)(DSu) + d(DSu)(DSv) =$$

$$= e^{\lambda r}uDv + vD(e^{\lambda r}u) + d[D(e^{\lambda r}u)](Dv) =$$

$$= e^{\lambda r}[uDv + vDu + d(Du)(Dv)] =$$

$$= e^{\lambda r}[uDv + \lambda vu + \lambda du\ Dv] =$$

*Observe that from Equality (8.6) for $\lambda = 0$ we obtain $Sz = z$ for all $z \in Z_D$.

$$= e^{\lambda r}[(1 + \lambda d)uDv + \lambda uv].$$

On the other hand, we have

$$SDx = SD(uv) = S[uDv + vDu + d(Du)(Dv)] = S[uDv + \lambda uv + \lambda duDv] =$$

$$= S[(1 + \lambda d)uDv + \lambda uv] = (1 + \lambda d)(Su)(SDv) + \lambda(Su)(Sv) =$$

$$= (1 + \lambda d)e^{r\lambda}uDv + \lambda e^{r\lambda}uv = e^{\lambda r}[(1 + \lambda d)uDv + \lambda uv] = DSx.$$

Thus Equality (8.5) holds on the set X_o in an arbitrary QL-ring X.

Suppose now that X is a Dh-ring, i.e. D satisfies condition (8.4). Then

$$Dx = D(uv) = uDv + f_1(u)Dx + f_2(v)Du + g_1(u)v + g_2(v)u =$$

$$= uDv + f_1(u)Dv + \lambda f_2(v)u + g_1(u)v + g_2(v)u.$$

Since $f_1(u)$, $f_2(v)$, $g_1(u)$, $g_2(v)$, as values of functionals, are scalars, we find

$$SDx = S(uDv) + f_1(u)SDv + \lambda f_2(v)Su + g_1(u)Sv + g_2(v)Su$$

$$= (Su)(SDv) + f_1(u)Dv + \lambda e^{\lambda r}f_2(v)u + g_1(u)v + e^{\lambda r}g_2(v)u$$

$$= e^{\lambda r}uDv + f_1(u)Dv + e^{\lambda r}[\lambda f_2(v) + g_2(v)]u + g_1(u)v.$$

On the other hand,

$$DSx = D[S(uv)] = D[(Su)(Sv)] = D(e^{\lambda r}uv) =$$

$$= e^{\lambda r}D(uv) = e^{\lambda r}[uDv + f_1(u)Dv + \lambda f_2(v)u + g_1(u)v + g_2(v)u] =$$

$$= e^{\lambda r}uDv + e^{\lambda r}g_1(u)v + e^{\lambda r}f_1(u)Dv + e^{\lambda r}[\lambda f_2(v) + g_2(v)]u.$$

Thus SDx = DSx if and only if

$$e^{\lambda r}uDv + f_1(u)Dv + g_1(u)v + e^{\lambda r}[\lambda f_2(v) + g_2(v)]u =$$

$$= e^{\lambda r}uDv + e^{\lambda r}g_1(u)v + e^{\lambda r}f_1(u)Dv + e^{\lambda r}[\lambda f_2(v) + g_2(v)],$$

i.e. if

$$f_1(u) = 0, \quad g_1(u) = 0.$$

The arbitrariness of $x = uv$ implies that $f_1 = g_1 = 0$.

Thus Condition (8.4) is of the form

$$D(xy) = xDy + f_2(y)Dx + g_2(y)x \quad \text{for all} \quad x,y \in \mathscr{D}_D. \tag{8.9}$$

The commutativity of the ring X implies that a condition dual to Condition (8.9) holds:

$$D(yx) = yDx + f_2(x)Dy + g_2(x)y \quad \text{for all} \quad x,y \in \mathscr{D}_D. \tag{8.10}$$

If we apply this condition to the element $x = uv$ in the same way as before, then we find:

$$SD(vu) = \lambda e^{\lambda r} vu + f_2(u)Dv + g_2(u)v ,$$

$$DS(uv) = \lambda e^{\lambda r} vu + e^{\lambda r} f_2(u)Dv + e^{\lambda r} g_2(u)v,$$

which implies that

$$f_2(u) = 0, \quad g_2(u) = 0$$

and we conclude that $f_2 = g_2 = 0$, i.e. X is a Dh_o-ring.

The following theorem permits the characterization of S^N-periodic elements by S-periodic elements.

Theorem 8.2. Suppose that X is a commutative linear ring over $\mathbb{C}$, $D \in R(X)$, $\dim Z_D \neq 0$, there exists $R \in \mathscr{R}_D V(X)$ and that exponential elements are not divisors of zero.* Suppose moreover, that the operator S_h is a D-shift on $h \in \mathbb{R}$, $\dim X_{S,N} > 0$ and that S_h is multiplicative: $S(xy) = (Sx)(Sy)$ for $x,y \in X$. Then $u \in X_j$ if and only if

$$u = e_{-\lambda}(z)v, \quad \text{where } Sv = v, \lambda = \frac{2\pi i}{Nh} j, \ e_\lambda = (I - \lambda R)^{-1} \quad \text{for } \lambda \in \mathbb{C}. \tag{8.11}$$

---

*This assumption is satisfied, for instance, in L-rings because in this case exponential elements are invertible: $[e_\lambda(z)]^{-1} = e_{-\lambda}(z)$ for $0 \neq z \in Z_D$, $\lambda \in \mathbb{C}$. In Dh_o-rings this assumption is satisfied because $\dim Z_D \neq 0$ (cf. Proposition 5 in [10]).

$(j = 1,2,\ldots,N)$, i.e. a general form of S^N-periodic elements is

$$x = \sum_{j=1}^{N} e_{2\pi ij/Nh}(z_j)v_j, \quad \text{where} \quad z_j \in Z_D, \quad Sv_j = v_j \tag{8.12}$$

$$(j = 1,\ldots,N).$$

Proof: If $u \in X_j$ then $Su = \varepsilon^j u$ $(j = 1,\ldots,N)$, where $\varepsilon = e^{2\pi i/N}$. Hence $\varepsilon^j u = Su = S[e_{-\lambda}(z)v] = [Se_{-\lambda}(z)]Sv = e^{\lambda h}e_{-\lambda}(z)Sv =$ $= e^{2\pi ijh/Nh}e_{-\lambda}(z)Sv = e^{2\pi ij/N}e_{-\lambda}(z)Sv = \varepsilon^j e_{-\lambda}(z)Sv$ for all $z \in Z_D$ and $e_{-\lambda}(z)Sv = e_{-\lambda}(z)v$ for all $z \in Z_D$, which implies $e_{-\lambda}(z)(v-Sv) = 0$. The arbitrariness of $z \in Z_D \neq 0$ and the assumption that exponential elements are not divisors of zero together imply that $Sv = v$.

On the other hand, if $Sv = v$ and u is of the form (8.11) then $Su = S[e_{-\lambda}(z)v] = [Se_{-\lambda}(z)]Sv = e^{\lambda h}e_{-\lambda}(z)v = e^{2\pi ijh/Nh}e_{-\lambda}(z)v =$ $= \varepsilon^j u$. Thus, $u \in X_j$ $(j = 1,\ldots,N)$.

<u>Proposition 8.1.</u> Suppose that X is a linear space over, $D \in R(X)$, $\dim D \neq 0$ and S_h is a D-shift on $0 \neq h \in \mathbb{R}$. Write:

$$Q(D) = \sum_{k=0}^{N} Q_k D^k, \quad \text{where } Q_k \in L_0(X), \text{ are S-periodic.} \tag{8.13}$$

If $x \in \ker Q(D)$ then $S_h^n x \in \ker Q(D)$ for an arbitrary positive integer n.

Indeed, if $x \in \ker Q(D)$ then $Q(D)x = 0$. Thus, by our assumptions, for $n = 1,2,\ldots$

$$Q(D)S_h^n x = \sum_{k=0}^{N} Q_k D^k S_h^n x = \sum_{k=0}^{N} Q_k S_h^n D^k x = \sum_{k=0}^{N} S_h^n Q_k D^k x =$$

$$= S_h^n \sum_{k=0}^{N} Q_k D^k x = S_h^n Q(D)x = 0.$$

Proposition 8.2. Suppose that X is a commutative linear ring, $D \in R(X)$, $\dim Z_D \neq 0$, S_h is a multiplicative D-shift on $0 \neq h \in \mathbb{R}$ and the polynomial Q(D) is as defined in Proposition 8.1. Suppose, moreover, that $u = e_\lambda(z)v$, where $z \in Z_D$, $v \in \mathscr{D}_D^N$ is an S^n-periodic element $(n \geqslant 1)$ and $u \in \ker Q(D)$. Then

$$\lambda = \frac{2\pi i}{nh} k \ , \quad k = 0, \pm 1, \pm 2, \ldots$$

Indeed, by our assumption and Proposition 8.1 we have $Q(D)u = 0$ and

$$0 = S^n Q(D)u = Q(D)S^n u = Q(D)S^n[e_\lambda(z)v] =$$

$$= Q(D)[S^n e_\lambda(z)](S^n v) = Q(D)[e^{-\lambda nh} e_\lambda(z)]v =$$

$$= e^{-\lambda nh} Q(D)[e_\lambda(z)v] = e^{-\lambda nh} Q(D)u.$$

This implies that $e^{-\lambda nh} = 1$, i.e. λ is of the required form.

Proposition 8.3. Suppose that all assumptions of Proposition 8.2 are satisfied. Suppose moreover that X is an L-ring. Then $Q(D + \lambda I)v = 0$, where λ is determined in Proposition 8.2. Conversely, if $Q(D + \lambda I)v = 0$, then $u = ve_\lambda(z) \in \ker Q(D)$.

Proof: Since $De_\lambda(z) = \lambda e_\lambda(z)$, we have

$$Du = D[ve_\lambda(z)] = (Dv + \lambda v)e_\lambda(z) = [(D + \lambda I)v]e_\lambda(z).$$

By an easy induction we find for $k = 1,2,\ldots$

$$D^k u = D^k[ve_\lambda(z)] = [(D + \lambda I)^k v]e_\lambda(z).$$

This implies that

$$0 = Q(D)u = \sum_{k=0}^{N} Q_k D^k u = \sum_{k=0}^{N} Q_k D^k [e_\lambda(z)v] =$$

$$= \sum_{k=0}^{N} Q_k [(D + \lambda I)^k v]e_\lambda(z) = [Q(D + \lambda I)v]e_\lambda(z).$$

Since X is an L-ring, exponential elements are not divisors of zero and we conclude that $Q(D + \lambda I)v = 0$. The sufficiency of the condition is obvious.

A similar statement can be proved for Dh_o-rings and QL-rings.

<u>Theorem 8.3.</u> Suppose that $D \in R(X)$, where X is either QL-ring (in particular: L-ring) or a Dh_o-ring. Suppose, moreover, that $\dim Z_D \neq 0$, there is an $R \in \mathscr{R}_D \cap V(X)$ and that $S_h \in L_o(X)$ is a multiplicative D-shift on $0 \neq h \in \mathbb{R}$. Write:

$$X_{EP}(\lambda_1,\ldots,\lambda_M) = \{x = \sum_{m=1}^{M} e_{\lambda_m}(z_m)v_m : v_m \in X,\ Sv_m = v_m,$$

$$z_m \in Z_D,\ \lambda_m \in \mathbb{C},\ \lambda_m \neq \lambda_j + 2\pi ik/h \text{ for } m \neq j, \tag{8.14}$$

$$k = 0,\pm1,\pm2,\ldots,\quad (j,m = 1,\ldots,M)\}$$

(M is an arbitrarily fixed positive integer). Then S_h is an algebraic operator on the space $X_{EP}(\lambda_1,\ldots,\lambda_M)$ with the characteristic polynomial

$$P(t) = \prod_{m=1}^{M} (t-t_m), \quad \text{where} \quad t_m = e^{-\lambda_m h} \quad (m = 1,\ldots,M).$$

(with single roots).

Proof: Suppose that $x = \Sigma_{m=1}^{M} e_{\lambda_m}(z_m)v_m \in X_{EP}(\lambda_1,\ldots,\lambda_m)$ is arbitrarily fixed. Then, by our assumptions,

$$S_h x = \sum_{m=1}^{M} S_h[e_{\lambda_m}(z_m)v_m] = \sum_{m=1}^{M} [S_h e_{\lambda_m}(z_m)](S_h v_m) =$$

$$= \sum_{m=1}^{M} e^{-\lambda_m h} e_{\lambda_m}(z_m)v_m .$$

By an easy induction we can show that

$$S_h^k x = S_h^k \sum_{m=1}^{M} e_{\lambda_m}(z_m)v_m = \sum_{m=1}^{M} t_m^k e_{\lambda_m}(z_m)v_m,$$

where $t_m = e^{-\lambda_m h}$ $(m = 1,2,\ldots,M;\ k = 0,1,2,\ldots)$.
If we write: $P(t) = \Pi_{m=1}^{M} (t-t_m) = \Sigma_{k=1}^{M} p_k t^k$, where $p_M = 1$, then we have $P(t_m) = 0$ for $m = 1,2,\ldots,M$.
Thus

$$P(S_h)x = \sum_{k=1}^{M} p_k S_h^k x = \sum_{k=1}^{M} p_k \sum_{m=1}^{M} t_m^k e_{\lambda_m}(z_m)v_m =$$

$$= \sum_{m=1}^{M} \Big(\sum_{k=1}^{M} p_k t_m^k\Big) e_{\lambda_m}(z_m)v_m = \sum_{m=1}^{M} P(t_m) e_{\lambda_m}(z_m)v_m = 0.$$

The arbitrariness of $x \in X_{EP}(\lambda_1,\ldots,\lambda_M)$ implies that $P(S_h) = 0$ on $X_{EP}(\lambda_1,\ldots,\lambda_M)$. The roots of the polynomial are single because we have assumed that $\lambda_m \neq \lambda_j + 2\pi ik/h$ for $m \neq j$, $k = 0,\pm 1,\pm 2,\ldots$, which implies that $t_m \neq t_j$ for $m \neq j$ $(j,m = 1,\ldots,M)$.

Corollary 8.1. Suppose that all assumptions of Theorem 8.3 are satisfied. Then the space $X_{EP}(\lambda_1,\ldots,\lambda_M)$ is direct sum of the eigenspaces of the operator S_h corresponding to the eigenvalues $t_1,\ldots,t_M$;

$$X_{EP}(\lambda_1,\ldots,\lambda_M) = \bigoplus_{m=1}^{M} X_m, \quad \text{where} \quad X_m = P_m X, \tag{8.15}$$

$$P_m = P_m(S_h), \; P_m(t) = \prod_{j=1, j\neq m}^{M} \frac{t-t_j}{t_m - t_j} \quad (m = 1,\ldots,M). \tag{8.16}$$

It is an immediate consequence of the fact that the operator S_h is algebraic on the space $X_{EP}(\lambda_1,\ldots,\lambda_M)$ and that its characteristic polynomial has single roots only.

The following corollary corresponds to Theorem 8.2:

Corollary 8.2. Suppose that all assumptions of Theorem 8.3 are satisfied. Then $x \in X_m$, where the spaces X_m are defined by Formulae (8.15)-(8.16), $(m = 1,2,\ldots,M)$ if and only if

$$x = e_{\mu_m}(z)v, \text{ where } z \in Z_D,\ S_h v = v \text{ and } v \text{ is not a divisor of zero}^* \tag{8.17}$$

$$\mu_m = \lambda_m + \frac{2\pi i}{h} j,\ j = 0, \pm 1, \pm 2,\ldots \quad (m = 1,2,\ldots,M).$$

---

* cf. the footnote on p. 116.

Proof: Suppose that x is of the form (8.17) for an m $(m = 1,2,\dots,M)$. Then

$$S_h x = S_h[e_{\mu_m}(z)v] = [S_h e_{\mu_m}(z)](S_h v) = e^{-\mu_m h} e_{\mu_m}(z)v =$$

$$= e^{-\lambda_m h+2\pi ij} e_{\mu_m}(z)v = e^{-\lambda_m h} e^{2\pi ij} e_{\mu_m}(z)v = t_m e_{\mu_m}(z)v = t_m x$$

which implies that $x \in X_m$. Conversely, suppose that $x \in X_m$ and $x = uv$, where $S_h v = v$ and v is not a divisor of zero. Since $t_m x = S_h x$, we find $t_m uv = t_m x = S_h x = S_h(uv) = (S_h u)(S_h v) = (S_h u)v$ which implies that

$$S_h u = t_m u = e^{-\lambda_m h} u = e^{-\lambda_m h+2\pi ij} u = e^{-\mu_m h} u.$$

Since S_h is a D-shift we conclude that $u = e_{\mu_m}(z)$ for a $z \in Z_D$.

<u>Corollary 8.3.</u> Suppose that all assumptions of Theorem 8.3 are satisfied. Write (as in Theorem 2.2):

$$Q_m(S_h) = \sum_{k=0}^{N-1} Q_{km} S_h^k, \quad Q(D,S_h) = \sum_{m=0}^{M} Q_m(S_h) D^{m+M_1} \tag{8.18}$$

where $M_1 \geqslant 0$, $Q_{km} \in L_0(X)$ are S_h-periodic $(m = 0,1,\dots,M;$ $k = 0,1,\dots,N-1)$. Then the equation

$$Q(D,S_h)x = y, \quad y \in X_{EP}(\lambda_1,\dots,\lambda_M) \tag{8.19}$$

has a solution $x \in X_{EP}(\lambda_1,\dots,\lambda_M)$ if and only if each of the independent equations

$$Q(D,t_j)x_j = y_j, \quad \text{where} \quad y_j = P_j y \ (j = 1,\dots,M), \tag{8.20}$$

and P_j are defined by Formula (8.16), has a solution $x_j \in X_j = P_jX$. If this condition is satisfied then $x = \Sigma_{j=1}^{M} x_j$.

Proof: Observe that the operators P_j, as polynomials with scalar coefficients in S_h, commute with the operator D. Thus $DX_j \subset X_j$ for $j = 1,2,\dots,M$. Since the space X is a direct sum of spaces $X_j = P_jX$ $(j = 1,2,\dots,N)$, we can write: $x = x_1 + \dots + x_M$, $y = y_1 + \dots + y_M$, where $x_j = P_jx$ and $y_j = P_jy$ and, moreover, $S_hx_j = t_jx$, $S_hy_j = t_jy$ for $j = 1,\dots,M$. Thus we have:

$$Q(D,S_h)x = \sum_{m=0}^{M} Q_m(S_h)D^{m+M_1}x = \sum_{m=0}^{M}\sum_{k=0}^{N-1} Q_{km}S_h^kD^{m+M_1}x =$$

$$= \sum_{m=0}^{M}\sum_{k=0}^{N-1} Q_{km}S_h^kD^{m+M_1}\sum_{j=1}^{M} x_j = \sum_{m=0}^{M}\sum_{k=0}^{N-1} Q_{km}D^{m+M_1}\sum_{j=1}^{M} S_h^kx_j =$$

$$= \sum_{m=0}^{M}\sum_{k=0}^{N-1} Q_{km}D^{m+M_1}\sum_{j=1}^{M} t_j^kx_j = \sum_{m=0}^{M}\sum_{j=1}^{M}\left(\sum_{k=0}^{N-1} Q_{km}t_j^k\right)D^{m+M_1}x_j =$$

$$= \sum_{m=0}^{M}\sum_{j=1}^{M} Q_m(t_j)D^{m+M_1}x_j = \sum_{j=1}^{M}\left[\sum_{m=0}^{M} Q_m(t_j)D^{m+M_1}\right]x_j =$$

$$= \sum_{j=1}^{M} Q(D,t_j)x_j \ .$$

Since the space $X_{EP}(\lambda_1,\dots,\lambda_M)$ is a direct sum of spaces $X_1,\dots,X_m$, equation (8.19) is equal to the system of M independent equations (8.20). If each of equations (8.20) has a solution $x_j \in X_j$ $(j = 1,\dots,M)$ then the equation (8.19) has a solution $x = x_1 + \dots + x_M$ which, by definition, belongs to the space $X_{EP}(\lambda_1,\dots,\lambda_M)$. Conversely, if x is a solution of the equation (8.19) belonging to the space $X_{EP}(\lambda_1,\dots,\lambda_M)$ then $x_j = P_j x$ is a solution of the j-th equation (8.20) belonging to the space X_j $(j = 1,\dots,M)$.

Corollaries 8.2 and 8.3 together imply the following

Corollary 8.4. Suppose that all assumptions of Theorem 8.3. are satisfied. Suppose that the operator $Q(D,S_h)$ is defined by Formula (8.18) and that the equation (8.19) has a solution $x \in X_{EP}(\lambda_1,\dots,\lambda_M)$. Then

$$x = \sum_{m=0}^{m} e_{\lambda_m}(z_m)v_m, \text{ where } z_m \in Z_D,\ Sv_m = v_m \text{ and } v_m \tag{8.21}$$

are not divisors of zero, $\mu_m = \lambda_m + 2\pi ij/h$, $j = 0,\pm 1,\pm 2,\dots$ $(m = 1,2,\dots,M)$.

Theorem 8.3 and Corollaries 8.2 and 8.3 generalize results of Włodarska-Dymitruk for differential-difference equations [1] (cf. also the author [3]).

It is well-known (cf. Arscott [1], Ince [1]) that every linear ordinary differential equation with periodic coefficients has at least one exponential-periodic solution. In particular, the Mathieu equation, which is of order 2, has two such solutions with known exponents and periodicity. We shall see that a similar theorem is true for polynomials in right invertible operators with periodic coefficients.

Theorem 8.4. (Floquet theorem for right invertible operators). Suppose that $D \in R(X)$, X is an L-ring, $\dim Z_D \neq 0$, F is an initial operator for an $R \in \mathscr{R}_D \cap V(X)$, $S_h \in L_0(X)$ is a multiplicative D-invariant D-shift and R-shift on $0 \neq h \in \mathbb{R}$ simultaneously, D_1, F_1, R_1^o are defined by Formulae (3.13), (3.20), $Q(D)$ is defined by Formula (8.13). Write:

$$\tilde{Q}_k = \sum_{m=k}^{N} \binom{m}{k} \lambda^{m-k} Q_m \quad (k = 0,1,\ldots,N) \tag{8.22}$$

$$\tilde{Q}(t,s) = \sum_{k=0}^{N} \tilde{Q}_k t^k s^{N-k}, \quad \tilde{Q}(t) = \tilde{Q}(t,1). \tag{8.23}$$

If the operator $\tilde{Q}(I,R_1^o)$ is invertible in the space $X_{S_h,1}$ then the equation

$$Q(D)x = 0 \tag{8.24}$$

has exponential-periodic solutions which are of the form

$$x = e_\lambda(z)v, \quad \text{where } S_h v = v, \ \lambda = \frac{2\pi i}{h} k \quad (k = 0,\pm 1,\pm 2,\ldots) \tag{8.25}$$

$$v = (R_1^o)^N [\tilde{Q}(I,R_1^o)]^{-1} \sum_{k=1}^{N} \tilde{Q}_k \sum_{j=0}^{k-1} (-1)^{k-j} h^{-k+j} z_j, \tag{8.26}$$

$z_o, z_1, \ldots, z_N \in Z_D$ are arbitrary.

Proof: Proposition 8.3 implies that Equation (8.24) has an exponential-periodic solution of the form (8.25) if and only if

$\lambda = (2\pi i/h)k$ $(k = 0,\pm 1,\pm 2,\ldots)$ and v satisfies the equation

$$Q(D + \lambda I)v = 0. \tag{8.27}$$

But, according with our notation (8.22), (8.23), we have

$$Q(D + \lambda I) = \sum_{m=0}^{N} Q_m (D + \lambda I)^m = \sum_{m=0}^{N} Q_m \sum_{k=0}^{m} \binom{m}{k} \lambda^{m-k} D^k =$$

$$= \sum_{k=0}^{N} \Big[\sum_{m=k}^{N} \binom{m}{k} \lambda^{m-k} Q_m\Big] D^k = \sum_{k=0}^{N} \tilde{Q}_k D^k = \tilde{Q}(D).$$

Observe that $\tilde{Q}_N = Q_N = I$ and that $\tilde{Q}_o,\ldots,\tilde{Q}_{N-1}$, as linear combinations of S_h-periodic operators, are again S_h-periodic. We can rewrite Equation (8.27) in the following way:

$$\tilde{Q}(D)v = 0. \tag{8.28}$$

Since the operator $\tilde{Q}(I,R_1^o)$ is invertible in the space $X_{S_h,1}$, Theorem 6.3 implies that Equation (8.28) has S_h-periodic solu tions which are of the form:

$$v = (R_1^o)^N [\tilde{Q}(I,R_1^o)]^{-1} \left(\sum_{k=1}^{N} \tilde{Q}_k \sum_{j=0}^{k-1} (-1)^{k-j-1} h^{-k+j} z_j\right) =$$

$$= (R_1^o)^N \, \tilde{Q}(I,R_1^o)^{-1} \sum_{k=1}^{N} \tilde{Q}_k \sum_{j=0}^{k-1} (-1)^{k-j} h^{-k+j} z_j$$

where $z_1,\ldots,z_N \in Z_D$ are arbitrary.

Corollary 8.5. Suppose that all assumptions of Theorem 8.4 are satisfied and that F is a multiplicative initial operator for D.

If $N = 2$ then there exist two exponential-periodic solutions x, y of Equation (8.24) such that

$$Fx = 0,\ FDx = x_1 \neq 0 \text{ and } Fy = y_o \neq 0,\ FDy = 0,$$
$$x_1, y_o \in Z_D. \tag{8.29}$$

Proof: Let $N = 2$. Then v is of the form:

$$v = (R_1^o)^2 [\tilde{Q}(I, R_1^o)]^{-1} [\tilde{Q}_1 z_o + \tilde{Q}_2 (h^{-2} z_o + h^{-1} z_1]. \tag{8.30}$$

Theorem 6.3 implies that

$$Fv = z_o, \quad FDv = z_1 . \tag{8.31}$$

This, our assumption that F is multiplicative and Liebniz Formula together imply that for $k = 0,1$ and $u = e_\lambda(z)v$ we have

$$FD^k u = FD^k [e_\lambda(z)v] = F \sum_{j=0}^{k} \binom{k}{j} [D^{k-j} e_\lambda(z)](D^j v) =$$

$$= \sum_{j=0}^{k} \binom{k}{j} [FD^{k-j} e_\lambda(z)](FD^j v) = \sum_{j=0}^{k} \binom{k}{j} \lambda^{k-j} [Fe_\lambda(z)] z_j =$$

$$= \sum_{j=0}^{k} \binom{k}{j} \lambda^{k-j} z z_j = z \sum_{j=0}^{k} \binom{k}{j} \lambda^{k-j} z_j .$$

Hence

$$Fu = z z_o \qquad FDu = \lambda z z_o + z z_1 .$$

Since z is arbitrary, we can admit $z \neq 0$. By our assumption that X is an L-ring z is not a divisor of zero. If we put $z_0 = 0$, $z_1 \neq 0$, we find an element $x = e_\lambda(z)v =$ $= e_\lambda(z)(R_1^o)^2[\tilde{Q}(I,R_1^o)]^{-1}h^{-1}\tilde{Q}_2 z_1$ such that $Fx = 0$, $FDx = zz_1 \neq 0$. Now, suppose that $z_0 \neq 0$ and $z_1 = -z_0$. Then $Fu = zz_o \neq 0$ and $FDu = \lambda zz_o - \lambda zz_o = 0$. Thus the element

$$y = e_\lambda(z)v = e_\lambda(z)(R_1^o)^2[\tilde{Q}(I,R_1^o)]^{-1}[\tilde{Q}_1 z_0 + \tilde{Q}_2(h^{-2}z_0 - h^{-1}\lambda z_0)] =$$

$$= h^{-2}e_\lambda(z)(R_1^o)^2[\tilde{Q}(I,R_1^o)]^{-1}[h^2\tilde{Q}_1 + (1-h\lambda)\tilde{Q}_2]z_0$$

has this property that $Fy \neq 0$, $FDy = 0$.

9 Polynomial - exponential - periodic elements

In this section we shall examine combinations of D-polynomials and exponential-periodic elements.

Theorem 9.1. Suppose that $D \in R(X)$, $R \in \mathscr{R}_D$ and S_h is an R-shift on h. Then for all positive integers k and n we have

$$S_h^n R^k z = \sum_{m=0}^{k} h_{k,m}^{(n)} R^m z \ , \quad \text{where} \quad z \in Z_D \tag{9.6}$$

$$h_{k,j}^{(1)} = \frac{(-1)^{k-j}}{(k-j)!} h^{k-j} \quad (j = 0,1,\ldots,k),\ n \geq 1. \tag{9.7}$$

$$h_{k,j}^{(n+1)} = \sum_{m=1}^{k} h_{k,m}^{(n)} h_{m,j}^{(1)} \ , \quad h_{k,k}^{(n+1)} = 1 \tag{9.8}$$

Proof, by induction. Let $z \in Z_D$ and a positive integer k be arbitrarily fixed. By definition (6.2) we have for $n = 1$

$$S_h R^k(z) = \sum_{j=0}^{k} \frac{(-1)^k}{(k-j)!} h^{k-j} R^j z = \sum_{j=0}^{k} h_{k,j}^{(1)} R^j z.$$

Suppose Formula (9.6) to be true for an arbitrarily fixed positive integer n. Then Formula (9.7) and (9.8) together imply that

$$S_h^{n+1} R^k z = S_h \sum_{m=0}^{k} h_{k,m}^{(n)} R^m z = \sum_{m=0}^{k} h_{k,m}^{(n)} S_h R^m z =$$

$$= \sum_{m=0}^{k} h_{k,m}^{(m)} \sum_{j=0}^{m} h_{m,j}^{(1)} R^j = \sum_{j=0}^{k} \left(\sum_{m=j}^{k} h_{k,m}^{(n)} h_{m,j}^{(1)} \right) R^j z = \sum_{j=0}^{k} h_{k,j}^{(n+1)} R^j z$$

which was to be proved. Moreover, by definition, $h_{k,k}^{(1)} = 1$. By an easy induction we can show that $h_{k,k}^{(n+1)} = h_{k,k}^{(n)} = h_{k,k}^{(1)} = 1$.

<u>Corollary 9.1.</u> Suppose that all assumptions of Theorem 9.1 are satisfied. Write:

$$P(t) = \sum_{m=0}^{M} P_m t^m, \quad \text{where } P_m \in \mathbb{C},\ P_M = 1, \tag{9.9}$$

M is an arbitrarily fixed positive integer. Then for an arbitrary integer n we have

$$S_h^n P(R) = \sum_{j=0}^{M} P_{M,j} R^j z, \quad \text{where} \tag{9.10}$$

$$P_{M,j} = \sum_{m=j}^{M} P_m h_{m,j}^{(n)} \quad (j = 0,1,\dots,M),\ P_{M,M} = 1, \tag{9.11}$$

where $h_{m,j}^{(n)}$ are defined by Formulae (9.7), (9.8).

Proof: Our assumptions and Theorem 9.1 together imply that for an arbitrary positive integer n we have

$$S_h^n P(R) z = S_h^n \sum_{m=0}^{M} P_m R^m z = \sum_{m=0}^{M} P_m S_h^n R^m z =$$

$$= \sum_{m=0}^{M} P_m \sum_{j=0}^{M} h_{m,j}^{(n)} R^j z = \sum_{j=0}^{M} \Big(\sum_{m=j}^{M} P_m h_{m,j}^{(n)}\Big) R^j z = \sum_{j=0}^{M} P_{M,j} R^j z$$

where $P_{M,j}$ are defined by Formulae (9.11). Since $h_{M,M}^{(n)} = 1$, $P_M = 1$, we find $P_{M,M} = P_M h_{M,M}^{(n)} = 1$.

<u>Corollary 9.2.</u> Suppose that all assumptions of Theorem 9.1 are

satisfied and that the polynomial P(t) is defined by Formula (9.9). Write

$$P^{(n+1)}(t) = \sum_{m=0}^{M} P_{M,n}t^{m},\ P^{(0)}(t) = P(t) \tag{9.12}$$

$$P_{M,m}^{(0)} = P_m,\ P_{M,m}^{(n+1)} = \sum_{m=j}^{M} P_{M,m}^{(n)}h_{m,j}^{(n)};\ P_{M,M}^{(n+1)} = 1 \tag{9.13}$$

$$(m = 0,1,\ldots,M;\ n = 0,1,2,\ldots)\ ,$$

where $h_{m,j}^{(n)}$ are defined by Formulae (9.7), (9.8). Then

$$S_h^n P^{(n)}(R)z = P^{(n+1)}(R)z \quad \text{for} \quad z \in Z_D \qquad (n = 0,1,2,\ldots). \tag{9.14}$$

Moreover,

$$P_{M,M}^{(n)} = 1 \quad \text{for} \quad M = 1,2,\ldots;\ n = 0,1,2,\ldots \tag{9.15}$$

Proof, by induction. Theorem 9.1 and Formulae (9.13) implies that

$$S_h^n P(R)z = \sum_{j=0}^{M} P_{M,j}R^j z = \sum_{j=0}^{M}\left(\sum_{m=j}^{M} P_m h_{m,j}^{(n)}\right)R^j z = \sum_{j=0}^{M} P_{M,j}^{(1)}R^j z = P^{(1)}(R)z$$

Suppose that Formula (9.14) is true for an arbitrarily fixed $n \geqslant 1$. Then, by Corollary 9.1 we find

$$S_h^n P^{(n+1)}(R) = S_h^n \sum_{m=0}^{M} P_{M,j}^{(n+1)}R^j = \sum_{j=0}^{M}\left(\sum_{m=j}^{M} P_{M,m}^{(n+1)}h_{m,j}^{(n)}\right)R^j z =$$

$$= \sum_{j=0}^{M} P_{M,j}^{(n+2)} R^j z = P^{(n+2)}(R)z.$$

Moreover, by definition, $P_{M,M}^{(0)} = P_{M,M} = 1$. Assume that $P_{M,M}^{(n+1)} = 1$ for an arbitrarily fixed $n \geq 1$. Then $P_{M,M}^{(n+2)} = P_{M,M}^{(n+1)} h_{M,M}^{(n)} = 1.1 = 1$, which was to be proved.

<u>Theorem 9.2.</u> Suppose that $D \in R(X)$, $R \in \mathscr{R}_D$ and S_h is an R-shift on h. Then for arbitrary positive integers n and k we have

$$(S_h - I)^{k+1} R^k z = 0 \quad \text{for all} \quad z \in Z_D . \tag{9.16}$$

Proof: Since by our assumptions S_h is an R-shift, we have

$$S_h z = z, \text{ i.e. } (S_h - I)z = 0 \quad \text{for all} \quad z \in Z_D . \tag{9.17}$$

Indeed, $S_h z = S_h R^o z = R^o z = z$ for all $z \in Z_D$. Put $n = 1$. Theorem 9.1 implies that for all $z \in Z_D$

$$(S_h - I)R^k z = \sum_{m=0}^{k} h_{k,m}^{(1)} R^m z - R^k z =$$

$$= \sum_{m=0}^{k-1} h_{k,m}^{(1)} R^m z = \sum_{m=0}^{k-1} \frac{(-1)^{k-m}}{(k-m)!} h^{k-m} R^m z$$

$$(S_h - I)^2 R^k z = (S_h - I) \sum_{m=0}^{k-1} h_{k,m}^{(1)} R^m z = \sum_{m=0}^{k-1} h_{k,m}^{(1)} (S_h - I) R^m z =$$

$$= h_{k,0}^{(1)} (S_h - I)z + \sum_{m=1}^{k-1} h_{k,m}^{(1)} \sum_{\nu=0}^{m-1} h_{m,\nu}^{(1)} R^\nu z =$$

$$= \sum_{\mu=0}^{k-2} h_{k,\mu+1}^{(1)} \sum_{\nu=0}^{\mu} h_{\mu+1,\nu}^{(1)} R^{\nu} z = \sum_{\nu=0}^{k-2} \left(\sum_{\mu=\nu}^{k-2} h_{k,\mu+1}^{(1)} h_{\mu+1,\nu}^{(1)} \right) R^{\nu} z.$$

Write:

$$\tilde{h}_{k,\nu}^{(j+1)} = \sum_{\mu=\nu}^{k-j} h_{k,\mu+j}^{(1)} h_{\mu+j,\nu}^{(1)} \qquad (9.18)$$

$$\text{for } j = 1,2,\ldots,k; \; \nu = 0,1,\ldots,k-j.$$

Then we can rewrite the last equality as follows:

$$(S_h - I)^2 R^k z = \sum_{\nu=0}^{k-2} \tilde{h}_{k,}^{(1)} R^{\nu} z \quad \text{for} \quad z \in Z_D \qquad (9.19)$$

In a similar way, acting by operator $S_h - I$ on the equality (9.19), after j steps $(j = 1,2,\ldots,k)$ we find

$$(S_h - I)^j R^k z = \sum_{\nu=0}^{k-j} \tilde{h}_{k,\nu}^{(j-1)} R^{\nu} z .$$

Thus

$$(S_h - I)^k R^k z = \tilde{h}_{k,0}^{(k-1)} z ,$$

and finally, using Formula (9.17)

$$(S_h - I)^{k+1} R^k z = (S_h - I) \tilde{h}_{k,0}^{(k-1)} z = \tilde{h}_{k,0}^{(k-1)} (S_h - I) z = 0 .$$

<u>Corollary 9.3.</u> Suppose that all assumptions of Theorem 9.2 are

satisfied. Then S_h is an algebraic operator on the space $P(R)$ with the characteristic polynomial $P(t) = (t-1)^{k+1}$ i.e. with one characteristic root $t = 1$ of multiplicity $k + 1$.

<u>Theorem 9.3.</u> Suppose that X is a commutative linear ring $D \in R(X)$, $R \in \mathscr{R}_D$ and that S_h is a multiplicative R-shift on h. Then for arbitrary positive integers k and N we have

$$(S_h^N - I)^{k+1}(vR^k z) = 0 \quad \text{for all} \quad z \in Z_D \text{ and } S_h^N\text{-periodic } v \in X \tag{9.20}$$

i.e. S_h is an algebriac operator on the space

$$\text{lin}\{vR^k z : z \in Z_D,\ S_h^N v = v,\ (k = 0,1,2,\ldots)\}$$

with the characteristic polynomial $P(t) = (t^N-1)^{k+1}$ and with the characteristic roots $\varepsilon^j = e^{2\pi ij/N}$ $(j = 0,1,\ldots,N-1)$, each of multiplicity $k + 1$.

Proof: Let N and k be arbitrarily fixed positive integers. Write: $u = vR^k z$. Then $S_h^N u = (S_h^N v)(S_h^N R^k z) = vS_h^N R^k z$, and $(S_h^N - I)u = vS_h^N R^k z - vR^k z = v(S_h^N - I)R^k z$. By an easy induction we can prove that

$$(S_h^N - I)^m (vR^k z) = v(S_h^N - I)^m R^k z \quad \text{for } m = 1,2,\ldots$$

$$(k = 0,1,2,\ldots) \tag{9.21}$$

$$z \in Z_D,\ S_h^N v = v\ .$$

This, and Theorem 9.2, together imply that

$$(S_h^N - I)^{k+1} u = v(S_h^N - I)^{k+1} R^k z = v(I + S_h + \ldots + S_h^{N-1})^{k+1} (S_h - I)^{k+1} R^k z = 0.$$

The arbitrariness of $z \in Z_D$ and v implies that S_h is an algebraic operator on the space under consideration with the characteristic polynomial $P(t) = (t^N - 1)^{k+1}$. Since all the N-th roots ε^j of unity are roots of the polymomial $t^N - 1$, we conclude that ε^j $(j = 0,1, \ldots, N-1)$ are roots of the polynomial P(t) with multiplicity k + 1.

Corollary 9.4. Suppose that all assumptions of Theorem 9.3 are satisfied. Write for arbitrarily fixed positive integers $M, n_o, \ldots, n_M$

$$X_{PP} = \{u = \sum_{m=0}^{M} v_m R^m z_m : z_m \quad Z_D,\ S_h^{n_m} v = v \ (m = 0,1,\ldots,M\} . \tag{9.22}$$

Then

$$P(S_h) = 0 \text{ on } X_{PP}, \text{ where } P(t) = \prod_{m=0}^{M} (t^{n_m} - I)^{M+1} \tag{9.23}$$

i.e. S_h is an algebraic operator on the space X_{PP} with the characteristic polynomial P(t). The polynomial P(t) has roots: $\varepsilon_m^j = e^{2\pi ij/n_m}$ $(m = 0,1,\ldots,M;\ j = 0,1,\ldots,n_m - 1)$ each of multiplicity M+1.

Proof: Suppose that $u = \Sigma_{m=0}^{M} v_m R^m z_m$, where $z_m \in Z_D$,

$S_h^{n_m}v_m = v_m$ $(m = 0,1,\ldots,M)$ is an arbitrary element of the space X_{pp} and that the polynomial $P(t)$ is defined by the second of Formulae (9.23). Theorem 9.3 implies that

$$P(S_h)u = [\prod_{m=0}^{M} (S_h^{n_m}-I)^{M+1}]\left(\sum_{k=0}^{M} v_k R^k z_k\right) = \sum_{k=0}^{M}\prod_{m=0}^{M} (S_h^{n_m}-I)^{M+1}]v_k R^k z_k =$$

$$= \sum_{k=0}^{M} [\prod_{m=0,m\neq k}^{M} (S_h^{n_m}-I)^{M+1}](S_h^{n_k}-I)^{M-k}[(S_h^{n_k}-I)^{k+1}v_k R^k z_k] = 0$$

The arbitrariness of $z_1,\ldots,z_M \in Z_D$ and $v_1,\ldots,v_M$ implies that $P(S_h) = 0$ on X_{PP}.

Corollary 9.5. Suppose that all assumptions of Theorem 9.3 are satisfied. Then the space X_{pp} of polynomial-periodic elements defined by Formula (9.22) is a direct sum of principial spaces X_{mj} corresponding to the eigenvalues

$\varepsilon_m^j = e^{2\pi ij/n_m}$ $(m = 0,1,\ldots,M;\ j = 0,1,\ldots,n_m-1)$, i.e. we have

$$X = \bigoplus_{\substack{j=1,\ldots,n_m-1\\ m=0,1,\ldots,M}} X_m, \text{ where } (S_h-\varepsilon_m^j I)^{M+1}\ x = 0 \quad \text{for} \quad x \in X_m. \tag{9.24}$$

It is an immediate consequence of the fact that S_h is an algebraic operator with characteristic roots of multiplicity M+1 on the space X_{PP}.

Theorem 9.4. Suppose that $D \in R(X)$, where X is either a QL-ring (in particular: L-ring) or Dh_o-ring. Suppose that $\dim Z_D \neq 0$ and there is an $R \in \mathscr{R}_D \cap V(X)$. Suppose moreover, that $S_h \in L_0(X)$ is a multiplicative D-shift on $h \neq 0$ and R-shift on h simultaneously. Write:

$$X_{PEP}(\lambda_j;K_j;N_j;M) =$$

$$= \{x = \sum_{j=0}^{M}\left(\sum_{k=0}^{K_j} v_{jk}R^k z_{jk}\right)e_{\lambda_j}(z_j) : z_{jk}, z_j \in Z_D, \tag{9.25}$$

$$v_{jk} \in X,\ S_h^{N_j} v_{jk} = v_{jk},\ \lambda_m \neq \lambda_j + 2\pi i l/n \quad \text{for } m \neq j;$$

$$l = 0,\pm 1,\pm 2,\ldots,;\ j = 0,1,\ldots,M;\ k = 0,1,\ldots,K_j\}$$

(M, K_j and N_j are arbitrarily fixed positive integers).

Then S_h is an algebraic operator on the space $X_{PEP}(\lambda_j;K_j;N_jM)$ with the characteristic polynomial

$$P(t) = \prod_{j=0}^{M}(t^{N_j} - t_j^{N_j})^{K_j+1}, \text{ where } t_j = e^{-\lambda_j h} \tag{9.26}$$

$$(j = 0,1,\ldots,M).$$

The polynomial P(t) has roots

$$t_{jm} = t_j\varepsilon_j^m, \text{ where } \varepsilon_j = e^{2\pi i/N_j} \tag{9.27}$$

$$(m = 0,1,\ldots,N_j-1;\ j = 0,1,\ldots,M)$$

of multiplicity K_j, respectively.

Proof: Suppose that $\lambda \in \mathbb{C}$, positive integers K and N and $z, \tilde{z} \in Z_D$ are arbitrarily fixed. Write:

$$(S_h^N - e^{-N\lambda h} I)^{K+1} w = 0, \text{ where } w = ve_\lambda(z)R^K\tilde{z},\ S_h^N v = v. \tag{9.28}$$

Indeed, in a similar way, as in the proof of Theorem 9.3, we obtain

$$S_h^N u = (S_h^N v)[S_h^N e_\lambda(z)]S_h^N R^k \tilde{z} = we^{-N\lambda h} e_\lambda(z) S_h^N R^K z$$

(because S_h is a multiplicative D-shift and R-shift simultaneously).

$$(S_h^N - e^{-N\lambda h} I)w = e^{-N\lambda h} ve_\lambda(z)(S_h^N - I)R^K z,$$

$$(S_h^N - e^{-N\lambda h} I)^{K+1} w = e^{-(K+1)N\lambda h} ve_\lambda(z)(S_h^N - I)^{K+1} R^k z = 0.$$

Suppose now that u is an arbitrary element of the space $X_{PEP}(\lambda_j;K_j;N;M)$, i.e. u is of the form

$$u = \sum_{j=0}^{M} \left(\sum_{k=0}^{K_j} v_{jk} R^k z_{jk} \right) e_{\lambda_j}(z_j)$$

where $M, K_j, N_j, \lambda_j, V_{jk}, Z_{jk}, z_j$ are described in Formula (9.25). The assumption $\lambda_m \neq \lambda_j + 2\pi il/h$ for $m \neq j$ asserts us that exponential elements $e_{\lambda_j}(z)$ are pairwise different and linearly independent. Suppose that the polynomial P(t) is defined by Formula (9.26). From Formula (9.28) we find

$$(S_h^{n_j} - e^{N_j \lambda_j h} I)^{k+1} v_{jk} e_{\lambda_j}(z_j) R^k z_{jk} = 0$$

$$\text{for } j = 0,1,\ldots,M;\ k = 0,1,\ldots,K_j .$$

Thus, in a similar way, as in the proof of Corollary 9.4 we obtain

$$P(S_h)u = [\prod_{j=0}^{M} (S_h^{N_j} - e^{N_j \lambda_j h} I)^{K_j+1}] \sum_{l=0}^{M} \sum_{k=0}^{K_l} v_{lk} e_{\lambda_l}(z_l) R^k z_{lk} =$$

$$= \sum_{l=0}^{M} \sum_{k=0}^{K_k} [\prod_{j=0}^{M} (S_h^{N_j} - e^{N_j \lambda_j h} I)^{K_j+1}] v_{lk} e_{\lambda_k}(z_l) R^k z_{lk} = 0$$

since $k \leqslant k_l$ $(l = 0,1,\ldots,M)$.

<u>Corollary 9.6.</u> Suppose that all assumptions of Theorem 9.4 are satisfied. Then the space $X_{PEP}(\lambda_j;K_j;N;M)$ is a direct sum of principal spaces X_{jm} corresponding to the eigenvalues t_{jm} $(m = 0,1,\ldots,N_j-1;\ j = 0,1,\ldots,M)$ of the operator S_h defined by Formula (9.27), i.e.

$$X = \bigoplus_{\substack{m=0,1,\ldots,N_j-1 \\ j=0,1,\ldots,M}} X_{jm} \tag{9.29}$$

where $(S_h - t_{jm})^{K_j+1} x = 0$ for $x \in X_{jm}$.

Theorem 9.4 and Corollary 9.6 could be easily generalized in the following way: we have assumed that elements v_{jk} are $S_h^{N_j}$-periodic, i.e. have the same periodicity for $k = 0,1,\ldots,K_j$. Now we can admit that an element v_{jk} is $S_h^{N_{jk}}$-periodic. The only difference will be that the characteristic polynomial has the form

$$P(t) = \prod_{j=0}^{K_j} (t^{n_{jk}} - e^{-N_{jk}\lambda_j h})^{K_j+1} . \qquad (9.30)$$

Corollary 9.7. Suppose that all assumptions of Theorem 9.2. are satisfied. Then a principal space corresponding to the root 1 of multiplicity k + 1 is of the form

$$\text{lin}\{R^k z : z \in Z_D, (k = 0,1,2,\ldots)\}.$$

Corollary 9.8. Suppose that all assumptions of Theorem 9.4 are satisfied and that N is an arbitrarily fixed positive integer. Then a principal space for the operator S_h corresponding to the root ε^j $(j = 0,1,\ldots,N-1)$, $\varepsilon = e^{2\pi i/N}$ of multiplicity k + 1 is of the form

$$X_j = \{e_\lambda(z) \sum_{m=0}^{k} v_m R^m z_m : \lambda = -2\pi ij/Nh,\ v_m \in X_1$$
$$S_h v_m = v_m, z,\ z_m \in Z_D,\ (m = 0,1,\ldots,k)\}. \qquad (9.31)$$

Proof: Since, by our assumption, S_h is a D-shift on h, we have for

$$S_h e_\lambda(z) = e^{-\lambda h} e_\lambda(z) = e^{-(-2\pi ij/Nh)h} e_\lambda(z) = e^{2\pi ij/N} e_\lambda(z) = \varepsilon^j e_\lambda(z),$$

i.e.

$$(S_h - \varepsilon^j I)e(z) = 0.$$

In the same way, as in the proof of Formula (9.28) we find

$$(S_h - \varepsilon^j I)^{m+1}[e_\lambda(z)v_m R^m z_m] = 0 \quad \text{for } m = 0,1,\ldots,k.$$

Thus

$$(S_h - \varepsilon^j I)^{k+1} e_\lambda(z) \sum_{m=0}^{k} v_m R^m z_m =$$

$$= \sum_{m=0}^{k} (S - \varepsilon^j I)^{k-m}(S - \varepsilon^j I)^{m+1}[e_\lambda(z)v_m R^m z_m] = 0.$$

This proves that every element of the form $x = e_\lambda(z)\,\Sigma_{m=0}^{k} v_m R^m z_m$

ε^j or multiplicity $k + 1$. Since we have $k + 1$ S_h-periodic coefficients $v_o,\ldots,v_k$ which are arbitrary, we conclude that the space X_j consists of all elements of this form.

<u>Corollary 9.9.</u> Suppose that all assumptions of Theorem 9.4 are satisfied. Then a principal space X_{jm} for the operator S_h corresponding to the root t_{jm} $(m = 0,1,\ldots,N_j-1;\ j = 0,1,\ldots,M)$ defined by Formula (9.27) of multiplicity $K_j + 1$ is of the form

$$X_{jm} =$$

$$= \{e_\tau(z) \sum_{\nu=0}^{K_j} v_\nu R^\nu z_\nu : \lambda = \lambda_j - 2\pi i m/N_h g,\ v_m \in X,\ S_h v \ = v\ ,$$

$$z,\ z_\nu \in Z_D\ (\ = 0,1,\ldots,K_j)\}\ (m = 0,1,\ldots,N_j-1;\ j = 0,1,\ldots,M). \tag{9.32}$$

Proof: By our assumptions we find for $z \in Z_D$

$$S_h e_\lambda(z) = e^{-\lambda h} e(z) = e^{-(\lambda_j - 2\pi i m/N_j h)h} e_\lambda(z) =$$

$$= e^{-\lambda_j h} e^{2\pi i m/N_j} e_\lambda(z) = e^{-\lambda_j h} \varepsilon_j^m e_\lambda(z) = t_{jm} e_\lambda(z) .$$

Further the proof proceeds on the same lines as the proof of Corollary 9.8.

Suppose that all assumptions of Theorem 9.4 are satisfied. Write, as before,

$$Q_m(S_h) = \sum_{k=0}^{N-1} Q_{km} S_h^k, \quad Q(D,S_h) = \sum_{m=0}^{M_1} Q_m(S_h) D^{m+M_2} , \tag{9.33}$$

where $M_2 \geqslant 0$, $Q_{km} \in L_o(X)$ are S_h-periodic $(m = 0,1,\dots,M_1;$ $k = 0,1,\dots,N-1)$.

<u>Theorem 9.5.</u> Suppose that all assumptions of Theorem 9.4 are satisfied, the operator $Q(D,S_h)$ is defined by Formulae (9.33) and the space $X = X_{PEP}(\lambda_j;K_j;N_j;M)$ is defined by Formulae (9.25). Then the equation

$$Q(D,S_h)x = y, \quad y \in X = X_{PEP}(\lambda_j;K_j;N_j;M) \tag{9.34}$$

has a solution in the space X if each of the equations

$$Q(D,S_h)x_{jm} = y_{jm}, \quad y_{jm} \in X_{jm}$$
$$(m = 0,1,\dots,N_j-1;\ j = 0,1,\dots,M), \quad y = \sum_{j=0}^{M} \sum_{m=0}^{N_j-1} y_{jm}, \tag{9.35}$$

where X_{jm} are principal spaces for S_h defined by Formula (9.32), has a solution $x_{jm} \in X_{jm}$. If this condition is satisfied then a solution of Equation (9.34) belonging to the space X is of the form $x = \Sigma_{j=0}^{M} \Sigma_{m=0}^{N_j-1} x_{jm}$. Conversely, if Equation (9.34) has a solution $x \in X$ then the (n,m)-equation (9.35) has a solution $x_{jm} \in X_{jm}$.

The proof is an immediate consequence of Corollary 9.6. Indeed, since the space X is a direct sum of spaces X_{jm}, we conclude that Equation (9.34) is equivalent to the system of $N = \Sigma_{j=0}^{M} N_j$ independent equations such that each of them is considered in one of the spaces X_{jm}.

An immediate consequence of Theorem 9.5 and Corollary 9.9 is

Corollary 9.10. Suppose that all assumptions of Theorem 9.5 are satisfied. Write:

$$y_{jm} = e_{\lambda_{jm}}(z_{jm}) \sum_{\nu=0}^{K_j} v_{jm\nu} R^{\nu} z_{jm\nu} \in X_{jm} \quad \text{where}$$

$$\lambda_{jm} = \lambda_j - 2\pi i m/N_j h, \quad v_{jm\nu} \in X,\ S_h v_{jm\nu} = v_{jm\nu}, \tag{9.36}$$

$z_{jm}, z_{jm\nu} \in Z_D$ $(\nu = 0,1,\ldots,K_j)$ X_{jm} are defined by

Formula (9.32), $(m = 0,1,\ldots,N_j-1;\ j = 0,1,\ldots,M)$.

$$y = \sum_{j=0}^{M} \sum_{m=0}^{N_j-1} y_{jm} \in X = X_{PEP}(\lambda_j; K_j; N_j; M). \tag{9.37}$$

If Equation (9.34) has a solution $x \in X$ then the (j,m)-equation (9.35) has a solution $x_{jm} \in X_{jm}$. Conversely, if each of Equations

(9.35) has a solution $x = \Sigma_{j=0}^{M} \Sigma_{m=0}^{N_j-1} x_{jm} \in X$.

Observe the following fact: since the space $X_{PEP}(\lambda_j;K_j;N_j;M)$ is a direct sum of spaces X_{jm} $(m = 0,1,\ldots,N_j-1;\ j = 0,1,\ldots,M)$, there exist $N = \Sigma_{j=1}^{M} N_j$ disjoint projectors P_{jm} giving a partition of unity and such that $P_{jm}X = X_{jm}$ (cf. the author [3] Theorem 4.1) i.e.

$$P_{jm}^2 = P_{jm},\ P_{jm} \neq P_{1k} \quad \text{for } j \neq 1 \text{ or } m \neq k,$$

$$\sum_{j=0}^{M} \sum_{m=0}^{N_j-1} P_{jm} = I \text{ and } (S_h - t_{jm}I)^{k_j+1} P_{jm} = 0$$

where t_{jm} are defined by Formula (9.27).

Results of this section generalize results of Włodarska-Dymitruk [1] for polynomial-periodic functions (cf. also the author [3]).

10 Equations with stationary coefficients

Suppose that $D \in R(X)$ $R \in \mathscr{R}_D$ an operator $A \in L_o(X)$ is said to be *stationary* if

$$DA - AD = 0 \text{ on } \mathscr{D}_D, \; RA - AR = 0. \tag{10.1}$$

Tasche [1] has considered linear equations with right invertible operators and with stationary coefficients in Banach spaces. Our considerations in linear spaces will be going in a slightly different way. Observe that, in particular, scalar matrices are stationary operators.

Proposition 10.1. If $A, B \in L_o(X)$ are stationary operators then $A + B$, AB and A are stationary operators for all $\lambda \in \mathscr{F}$.

Proof: By our assumptions, $DA - AD = 0$, $DB - BD = 0$, $RA - AR = 0$, $RB - BR = 0$, hence

$$D(A + B) - (A + B)D = DA + DB - AD - BD = 0;$$

$$D(AB) - (AB)D = DAB - ADB + ADB + ADB - ABD =$$

$$= (DA - AD)B + A(DB - BD) = 0;$$

$$D(\lambda A) - (\lambda A)D = \lambda(DA - AD) = 0.$$

A similar proof for commutators with R.

<u>Corollary 10.1.</u> Suppose that $D \in R(X)$ and $R \in \mathscr{R}_D$. The set $S_{D,R}$ of all stationary operators (i.e. of the set of all operators belonging to $L_0(X)$ and commuting with D and R) is a subring of the linear ring $L_0(X)$.

By an easy induction we can prove that

$$\text{if } A \in S_{D,R} \quad \text{then} \quad A^n \in S_{D,R} \quad \text{for all} \quad n \in \mathbb{N}. \tag{10.2}$$

<u>Theorem 10.1.</u> Suppose that $D \in R(X)$, $\dim Z_D \neq 0$, F is an initial operator for an $R \in \mathscr{R}_D$, $A \in S_{D,R}$ and the operator $I-RA = I-AR$ is invertible. Write:

$$E_A = (I-RA)^{-1} \tag{10.3}$$

Then

$$DE_A = AE_A + D \text{ on } \mathscr{D}_D, \text{ i.e. } (D-A)E_A = D \text{ on } \mathscr{D}_D; \tag{10.4}$$

$$FE_A = F; \tag{10.5}$$

$$(D-A)E_AF = 0. \tag{10.6}$$

Proof: Observe that on the domain of D we have the following equalities: $D-A = D-DRA = D(I-RA) = D(I-AR)$, which implies: $(D-A)E_A = (D-A)(I-AR)^{-1} = D(I-AR)(I-AR)^{-1} = D$, i.e. Formulae (10.4) hold. By our assumptions

$FE_A = (I-RD)E_A = E_A - RAE_A + D = E_A - RAE_A - RD(I-RA)E_A - RD =$ $(I-AR)(I-AR)^{-1}(I-RD) = I - RD = F$. Since $DF = 0$, we find $(D-A)E_AF = DF = 0$.

<u>Corollary 10.2.</u> Suppose that all assumptions of Theorem 10.1 are satisfied. Then

$$(D-A)E_Az = 0 \quad \text{and} \quad FE_Az = z \quad \text{for all } z \in Z_S . \tag{10.7}$$

Indeed, suppose that $z \in Z_D$ is arbitrary. Then $Fz = z$ and Formula (10.6) implies $0 = (D-A)E_AFz = (D-A)E_Az$. Formula (10.5) implies that $FE_Az = Fz = z$.

<u>Corollary 10.3.</u> Suppose that all assumptions of Theorem 10.1 are satisfied. Then all solutions of the equation

$$(D-A)x = y \tag{10.8}$$

are of the form

$$x = E_A(Ry+z), \text{ where } z \in Z_D \text{ is arbitrary.} \tag{10.9}$$

Indeed, write: $u = (I-AR)x$. Then $x = E_Au$. The second of Formulae (10.4) implies that $Du = (D-A)E_Au = (D-A)x = y$. Then $u = Ry + z$, where z is an arbitrary constant.

The definition of the operator E_A implies immediately

<u>Corollary 10.4.</u> Suppose that all assumptions of Theorem 10.1 are satisfied and that $A = \lambda I$, where $\lambda \in \mathscr{F}$. Then

$$E_{\lambda I}(z) = e_\lambda(z) \quad \text{for all} \quad z \in X_D \ (\lambda \in \mathscr{F}). \tag{10.10}$$

Corollaries 10.2 and 10.4 show that the operator E_A defined by means of Formula (10.3) is a generalization of the exponential operator e_λ .

For equations of higher order we obtain the following

Theorem 10. 2. Suppose that all assumptions of Theorem 10.1 are satisfied. Then the general solution of the equation

$$(D-A)^N x = y,\ y \in X \quad (N \geqslant 1) \tag{10.11}$$

is of the form

$$x = E_A^N (R^N y + \sum_{k=0}^{N-1} R^k z_k), \text{ where } z_o, \ldots, z_{N-1} \in Z_D \tag{10.12}$$

are arbitrary.

Proof: To begin with, we shall prove by induction that

$$D^k (I-AR)^k = (D-A)^k. \tag{10.13}$$

Indeed, for $k = 1$ we have $D(I-AR) = D-A$. Suppose Formula (10.13) to be true for an arbitrarily fixed positive integer k. Then

$$D^{k+1}(I-AR)^{k+1} = D[D^k(I-AR)^k](I-AR) = D(D-A)^k(I-AR) =$$

$$= (D-A)^k D(I-AR) = (D-A)^k(D-A) = (D-A)^{k+1}.$$

Thus Formula (10.13) is true for an arbitrary $k \in \mathbb{N}$. Write, as in the proof of Corollary 10.3, $u = (I-AR)^N x$. Then $x = E_A^N u$. Formulae (10.4) and (10.3) together imply that $D^N u = D^N (I-AR)^N x = (D-A)^N x = y$. Thus $u = R^N y + \Sigma_{k=0}^{N-1} R^k z_k$, where $z_0, \ldots, z_{N-1} \in Z_D$ are arbitrary. We therefore conclude that $E_A^N (R^N y + \Sigma_{k=0}^{N-1} R^k z_k)$, where $z_0, \ldots, z_{N-1} \in Z_D$ are arbitrary.

Theorem 10.3. Suppose that $D \in R(X)$, $\dim Z_D \neq 0$, F is an initial operator for an $R \in \mathscr{R}_D$, $A \in S_{D,R}$ and that the operators $I-iAR$, $I+iAR$ are invertible. Write:

$$C_A = \frac{1}{2}(E_{iA} + E_{-iA}), \ S_A = \frac{1}{2i}(E_{iA} - E_{-iA}). \tag{10.14}$$

The operators C_A and S_A have the following properties:

$$C_A = (I+A^2R^2)^{-1}, \ S_A = AR(I+A^2R^2)^{-1} = ARC_A; \tag{10.15}$$

$$DC_A = -AS_A + D \text{ on } \mathscr{D}_D; \ DS_A = AC_A; \tag{10.16}$$

$$(D^2+A^2)C_A = D^2 \quad \text{and} \quad (D^2+A^2)S_A = AD \quad \text{on } \mathscr{D}_D. \tag{10.17}$$

Moreover, every solution of the equation

$$(D^2+A^2)x = y, \ y \in X \tag{10.18}$$

is of the form

$$x = C_A R^2 y + C_A z_0 + S_A z_1, \quad \text{where } z_0, z_1 \in Z_D \text{ are arbitrary.}$$

Proof: By our assumptions the operator $I+A^2R^2 = (I-iAR)(I+iAR)$ is invertible, since it is a superposition of invertible operators. Then

$$C_A = \frac{1}{2}(E_{iA}+E_{-iA}) = \frac{1}{2}[(I-iAR)^{-1} + (I+iAR)^{-1}] =$$

$$= \frac{1}{2}(I+A^2R^2)^{-1}[I+iAR+I-iAR] = (I+A^2R^2)^{-1};$$

$$S_A = \frac{1}{2i}(E_{iA}-E_{-iA}) = \frac{1}{2}[(I-iAR)^{-1} - (I+iAR)^{-1}] =$$

$$= \frac{1}{2i}(I+A^2R^2)^{-1}[I+iAR-(I-iAR)] = \frac{1}{2i}\, 2iAR(I+A^2R^2)^{-1} =$$

$$= AR(I+A^2R^2)^{-1} = ARC_A.$$

The definition of the operator C_A and Property (10.4) together imply that on $\mathscr{D}_D$ we have

$$DC_A = \frac{1}{2}(DE_{iA}+DE_{-iA}) = \frac{1}{2}(iAE_{iA} - iAE_{-iA}+D+D) =$$

$$= \frac{1}{2}A(E_{iA}-E_{-iA})+D = -A\,\frac{1}{2i}(E_{iA}-R_{iA})+D = -AS_A+D.$$

The second of Equalities (10.5) implies that $DS_A = DARC_A = ADRC_A = AC_A$. The equalities (10.16) implies that on the domain of the operator D^2 we have

$$(D^2+A^2)C_A = D(DC_A) + A^2C_A = D(-AS_A+D) + A^2C_A =$$

$$= -ADS_A + D^2 + A^2C_A = -A^2C_A + D^2 + A^2C_A = D^2;$$

$$(D^2+A^2)S_A = D(DS_A) + A^2S_A = D(AC_A) + A^2S_A = ADC_A + A^2S_A =$$

$$= A(-AS_A+D)+A^2S_A = -A^2S_A + AD + A^2S_A = AD.$$

Consider now Equation (10.18). Write: $u = (I+A^2R^2)x$. Then $x = C_Au$. On the other hand, since $D^2u = D^2(I+A^2R^2)x = (D^2+A^2D^2R^2)x = (D^2+A^2)x = y$, we have $u = R^2y+z_0+Rz_o'$, where $z_0, z_0' \in Z_D$ are arbitrary. Thus $x = C_Au = C_A(R^2y+z_0+Rz_o')$. But, by our assumptions, $DA = AD$, which implies $A_{ZD} \subset Z_D$. We therefore can introduce a new constant $Az_1 \in Z_D$, where $z_1 \in Z_D$, instead of the constant z_0'. Since also $AR = RA$, we find $ARC_A = C_AAR$. Thus the second of Equalities (10.15) implies

$$x = C_A(R^2y+z_0Rz_o') = C_AR^2y+C_Az_o+C_ARAz_1 =$$

$$= C_AR^2y + C_Az_o + ARC_Az_1 = C_AR^2y + C_Az_o + S_Az_1, \quad \text{where}$$

$$z_0, z_1 \in Z_D$$

Observe that the operators C_A and S_A defined by means of Equalities (10.14) are generalizations of cosine and sine operators c_λ and s_λ. In particular we have

$$C_{\lambda I} = c_\lambda, \quad S_{\lambda I} = s_\lambda \quad \text{for all} \quad \lambda \in \mathscr{F}, \tag{10.19}$$

provided that R is a Volterra operator.

<u>Proposition 10.2.</u> Suppose that $D \in R(X)$, $\dim Z_D \neq 0$, $R \in \mathscr{R}_D$,

$A \in S_{D,R}$. Then

$$FA = AF \ . \tag{10.20}$$

Indeed, since AD = DA and RA = AR, we have $FA = (I-RD)A = A(I-RD) = AF$ on $\mathscr{D}_D$, which implies AF = FA.

<u>Theorem 10.4.</u> Suppose that X is a Banach space, $D \in R(X)$, $\dim Z_D \neq 0$ $R \in \mathscr{R}_D$, $A \in S_{D,R}$ is bounded and $S_h \in L_o(X)$ is a bounded R-shift on $0 \neq 0 \in \mathbb{R}$. If the set P(R) of all polynomials

$$AS_h = S_h A \ . \tag{10.21}$$

Proof: Since DA = AD we have $AZ_D \subset Z_D$ which implies that $Az \in Z_D$ for every $z \in Z_D$. Since S_h is an R-shift on h, we have for k = 0,1,2,.... and $z \in Z_D$.

$$AS_h R^k z = A \sum_{j=0}^{k} \frac{(-1)^{k-j}}{(k-j)!} h^{k-j} R^j z = \sum_{j=0}^{k} \frac{(-1)^{k-1}}{(k-j)!} h^{k-j} AR^j z =$$

$$= \sum_{j=0}^{k} \frac{(-1)^{k-j}}{(k-j)!} h^{k-j} R^j Az = S_h R^k Az = S_h AR^k z$$

which implies

$$(AS_h - S_h A)R^k z = 0 \quad \text{for all} \quad z \in Z_D \quad \text{and} \quad k = 0,1,2,\ldots$$

Since $\overline{P(R)} = X$, we conclude that $AS_h - S_h A = 0$.

Corollary 10.5. Suppose that all assumptions of Theorem 10.4 are satisfied. Then

(i) if the operator $I-AR$ is invertible then E_A is S_h-periodic:

$$S_h E_A = E_A S_h \tag{10.22}$$

(ii) if the operators $I-iAR$, $I+iAR$ are invertible then the operators C_A, S_A are S_h-periodic:

$$S_h C_A = C_A S_h \ , \quad S_h S_A = S_A S_h \ . \tag{10.23}$$

Proof: Formula (10.21) and our assumptions together imply that $S_h(I-AR) = (S_h - S_h AR) = S_h - AS_h R = S_h - ARS_h = (I-AR)S_h$. Then $S_h E_A = S_h(I-AR)^{-1} = (I-AR)^{-1}S_h = E_A S_h$. Formulae (10.4) imply that $S_h C_A = (1/2)S_h(E_{iA}+E_{-iA}) = (1/2)(E_{iA}+E_{-iA})S_h = C_A S_h$. A similar proof follows for the operator S_A.

Corollary 10.6. Suppose that all assumptions of Theorem 10.4 are satisfied and that the operators D_1 and R_1^o are defined by Formulae (3.13),(3.20):

$$D_1 = D - \frac{1}{h} FS_h , \ R_1^o = (I + FS_h + \frac{1}{h} RFS_h)R, \tag{10.24}$$

where F is an initial operator for D corresponding to R.

Then

$$D_1A = AD_1, \quad R_1^oA = AR_1^o . \tag{10.25}$$

Proof: Our assumptions, Formula (10.20) and Corollary 10.5 together imply that

$$D_1A = (D - \frac{1}{h} FS_h)A = DA - \frac{1}{h} FS_hA = AD - \frac{1}{h} FAS_h = AD - \frac{1}{h} AFS_h =$$

$$= A(D - \frac{1}{h} FS_h) = AD_1;$$

$$R_1^oA = (I + FS_h + \frac{1}{h} RFS_h)RA = (I + FS_h + \frac{1}{h} RFS_h)AR =$$

$$= (A + AFS_h + A\frac{1}{h} RFS_h)R = A(I + FS_h + \frac{1}{h} RFS_h)R = AR_1^o$$

<u>Corollary 10.7.</u> Suppose that all assumptions of Theorem 10.4 are satisfied, the operators D_1 and R_1^o are defined by Formulae (10.24) and the operators $I-AR$ and $I-A(R+R_1^o) = I-A(2I+FS_h + (1/h)RFS_h)R$ are invertible. Then the equation

$$Dx = Ax + y, \quad y \in X_{S_h,1} \tag{10.26}$$

has a unique S_h-periodic solution satisfying the condition

$$Fx = x_o \tag{10.27}$$

which is of the form

$$x = (I-AR-AR_1^o)^{-1}(R_1^oy - \frac{1}{h} x_o) . \tag{10.28}$$

Proof: Write: $u = (I-AR)x$. Then $x = E_A u$. Formula (10.20) implies that $Fu = Fx - FARx = Fx - AFRx = Fx = x_o$. Theorem 3.3, Formulae (3.21) and (10.4) together imply that

$$u = R_1^o D_1 u = R_1^o (Du - \frac{1}{h} Fu) = R_1^o [(D-A)E_A u - AE_A u - \frac{1}{h} x_o] =$$

$$= R_1^o [(D-A)x - AE_A u - \frac{1}{h} x_o] = R_1^o (y - \frac{1}{h} x_o - AE_A u) .$$

Hence

$$(I - R_1^o AE_A)u = R_1^o (y - \frac{1}{h} x_o) .$$

But, by Corollary 10.6,

$$I - R_1^o AE_A = I - AR_1^o (I-AR)^{-1} = (I-AR-AR_1^o)(I-AR)^{-1} =$$

$$= (I-AR-AR_1^o)E_A ,$$

and this operator is invertible as it is a superposition of invertible operators. Thus

$$u = (I-R_1^o AE_A)^{-1} R_1^o (y - \frac{1}{h} x_o) = E_A^{-1} (I-AR-AR_1^o)^{-1} (R_1^o y - \frac{1}{h} x_o)$$

and $x = E_A u = (I-AR-AR_1^o)^{-1}(R_1^o y - 1/h\ x_o)$. This solution is S_h-periodic because we were dealing in the space $X_{S_h,1}$ only (Theorem 3.3).

11 Shifts in linear rings

Suppose that X is a commutative linear ring over an algebraically closed field $\mathscr{F}$ and $D \in R(X)$.

Recall (cf. the author [10]) that X is a *quasi-Leibniz ring* (in short: *QL-ring*) if there exists a scalar d such that

$$D(xy) = xDy + yDx + d(Dx)(Dy) \quad \text{for all } x,y \in \mathscr{D}_D. \tag{11.1}$$

If d=0 then X is said to be a *Leibniz ring* (in short: L-ring). For instance, Formula (4.11) shows us that the linear ring X considered in Example 4.6 is an L-ring. X is a *simple Duhamel ring* (in short: *Dh_o-ring*) if

$$D(xy) = xDy \quad \text{for all } x,y \in \mathscr{D}_D . \tag{11.2}$$

In [10] we have considered Duhamel rings in a more general case.

In this section we shall study R-shifts and D-shifts in linear rings with unit e and we shall show that in some QL-rings and Dh_o-rings D-shifts exist even in the case when $R \notin V(X)$.

Proposition 11.1. Suppose that $D \in R(X)$ where X is an L-ring with unit e and F is an initial operator for D corresponding to an $R \in \mathscr{R}_D$. Then $De = 0$, $Fe = e$ and we have the following formula for *integration by parts*:

$$R(xDy) = xy - R(yDx) - F(xy) \quad \text{for all } x,y \in \mathscr{D}_D . \tag{11.3}$$

Proof: Let $x \in X$ be arbitrarily fixed. Then $Dx = D(ex) = xDe + eDx = xDe + Dx$ and $xDe = 0$. The arbitrariness of $x \in X$ implies $De = 0$. Since $De = 0$, we have: $e \in Z_D$ and $Fe = e$. By our assumptions we have: $D(xy) = xDy + yDx$ for all $x,y \in \mathscr{D}_D$. This yields the following equality:

$$xy = R(xDy) + R(yDx) + F(xy) \quad \text{for all } x,y \in \mathscr{D}_D.$$

<u>Theorem 11.1.</u> Suppose that $D \in R(X)$, where X is an L-ring with unit e and F is an initial operator for D corresponding to an $R \in \mathscr{R}_D$ and satisfying the following condition:

$$F(zx) = zFx \quad \text{for all } x \in X,\ z \in Z_D . \tag{11.4}$$

Then for all $z \in Z_D$ and $n \in \{0\} \cup \mathbb{N}$

$$F(zR^n e) = 0; \tag{11.5}$$

$$R^n z = zR^n e ; \tag{11.6}$$

and

$$R^n e = \frac{(Re)^n}{n!} - \sum_{k=2}^{n} \frac{1}{k!} R^{n-k} F[(Re)^k] \quad \text{for } n \geqslant 2 . \tag{11.7}$$

Proof: Since $FR = 0$ we have $F(zRx) = zFRx = 0$ for all $x \in X$, $z \in Z_D$ (putting Rx in Formula (11.4) instead of x). In particular, for an arbitrarily fixed non-negative integer n we find:

$F(zR^n e) = zFR^n e = 0$. Formula (11.3) for integration by parts implies that for all $z \in Z_D$ we have $Rz = R(ze) = zRe - R[(DzRe] - F(zRe) = zRe$, because $Dz = 0$ and $F(zRe) = 0$. Thus we already have Formula (11.6) for $n = 1$. Suppose Formula (11.6) to be true for an arbitrarily fixed positive integer n. Then, by our assumptions, we obtain

$$R^{n+1}z = R(R^n z) = R(zR^n e) =$$

$$= zR^{n+1}e - R[(Dz)(R^n e)] - F(zR^n e) = zR^{n+1}e$$

which has to be proved. In order to prove Formula (11.7) observe that by the Leibniz condition we have:

$$D[(Re)^2] = (DRe)(Re) + (Re)(DRe) = 2(DRe)Re = 2eRe = 2Re \ ,$$

which implies: $R^2 e = R(Re) = (Re)^2/2! + z$, where $z \in Z_D$. Since $FR = 0$ and $Fz = z$, we find $z = Fz = FR^2 e - (1/2!)F[(Re)^2] = -(1/2!)F[(Re)^2]$. This proves Formula (11.7) for $n = 2$. Suppose now Formula (11.7) to be true for an arbitrarily fixed positive integer $n \geqslant 2$. Write: $g = Re$, $u_n = -\Sigma_{k=2}^{n}(1/k!)R^{n-k}Fg^k$ for $n \geqslant 2$. Our induction assumption can be rewritten as follows:

$$R^n e = \frac{g^n}{n!} + u_n \quad \text{for } n \geqslant 2 \ . \tag{11.8}$$

We have

$$Dg^n = ng^{n-1} \quad \text{for} \quad n \in \mathbb{N}. \tag{11.9}$$

Indeed, $Dg = e$. Suppose Formula (11.9) to be true for an arbitrary positive integer n. Then $Dg^{n+1} = D(g \cdot g^n) = gDg^n + g^n Dg = g \cdot n\, g^{n-1} + g^n DRe = ng^n + g^n \cdot e = (n+1)g^n$, which proves that $Dg^n = ng^{n-1}$ for all $n \in \mathbb{N}$. Formula (11.9) implies that

$$Dg^{n+1} = (n+1)g^n, \quad g^{n+1} = (n+1)Rg^n + Fg^{n+1} \quad \text{and}$$

$$Rg^n = \frac{1}{n+1}(g^{n+1} - Fg^{n+1}) \; .$$

Then from Formula (11.8) we obtain

$$R^{n+1}e = R(\frac{g^n}{n!} + u_n) = \frac{Rg^n}{n!} + Ru_n =$$

$$= \frac{1}{(n+1)n!} (g^{n+1} - Fg^{n+1}) - R \sum_{k=2}^{n} \frac{1}{k!} R^{n-k}Fg^k =$$

$$= \frac{g^{n+1}}{(n+1)!} - \frac{1}{(n+1)!} Fg^{n+1} - \sum_{k=2}^{n} \frac{1}{k!} R^{n+1-k}Fg^k =$$

$$= \frac{g^{n+1}}{(n+1)!} - \sum_{k=2}^{n+1} \frac{1}{k!} R^{n+1-k}Fg^k =$$

$$= \frac{g^{n+1}}{(n+1)!} + u_{n+1}$$

This proves Formula (11.7) for all $n \geq 2$.

Corollary 11.1. Suppose that $D \in R(X)$, where X is an L-ring with unit e and F is a *multiplicative* initial operator for D

corresponding to an $R \in \mathscr{R}_D$, i.e. $F(xy) = (Fx)(Fy)$ for all $x,y \in X$. Then Formulae (11.5) and (11.6) hold and, moreover,

$$R^n e = \frac{(Re)^n}{n!} \text{ for all } n \in \mathbb{N}. \tag{11.10}$$

Proof: The proofs of Formulae (11.5) and (11.6) are exactly the same as before. In order to prove Formula (11.10) it is sufficient to observe that $F[(Re)^n] = F[(Re)][F(Re)^{n-1}] = (FRe)F[(Re)^{n-1}] = 0$ for all $n \geq 1$, since F is a multiplicative operator.

We should point out that Formula (11.10) has been recently obtained by H. von Trotha (cf. Example 4.6).

<u>Theorem 11.2.</u> Suppose that all assumptions of Theorem 11.1 are satisfied. Suppose, moreover, that $\mathscr{F} = \mathbb{C}$, X is a Banach algebra (with respect to the structure operations under consideration) and the operators F and R are bounded. Consider the series

$$\sum_{n=0}^{\infty} \lambda^n R^n e \tag{11.11}$$

Then (provided that $\| e \| = 1$)

1° If $|\lambda| < 1/\| R \|$ then the series (11.11) is convergent, exponential elements exist and are of the form

$$e_\lambda(z) = z \sum_{n=0}^{\infty} \lambda^n R^n e \quad \text{for} \quad |\lambda| < \frac{1}{\| R \|}, \; z \in Z_D. \tag{11.12}$$

2° If the operator F is multiplicative, then the series (11.11) is convergent for all $\lambda \in \mathbb{C}$, exponential elements exist for all $\lambda \in \mathbb{C}$ and are of the form (11.12).

Proof: For all $n \in \mathbb{N}$ we have the following estimation:

$$\| \sum_{k=0}^{n} \lambda^k R^k e \| = \| \sum_{k=0}^{n} \lambda^k (\frac{(Re)^k}{k!} - \sum_{j=2}^{k} \frac{1}{j!} R^{k-j} F[(Re)^j]) \| \leqslant$$

$$\leqslant \sum_{k=0}^{n} |\lambda|^k (\frac{\| R \|^k}{n!} + \sum_{j=2}^{k} \frac{1}{j!} \| R \|^{k-j} \| F \| \cdot \| R \|^j) =$$

$$= \sum_{k=0}^{n} |\lambda|^k (\frac{\| R \|^k}{k!} + \sum_{j=2}^{k} \frac{1}{j!} \| R \|^k \| F \|) =$$

$$= \sum_{k=0}^{n} |\lambda|^k \| R^k \| (\frac{1}{k!} + \| F \| \sum_{j=2}^{k} \frac{1}{j!})$$

$$\leqslant \sum_{k=0}^{n} |\lambda|^k \| R \|^k \cdot \frac{1}{k!} + \| F \| \sum_{k=0}^{n} |\lambda|^k \| R \|^k \sum_{j=2}^{k} \frac{1}{j!}$$

$$\leqslant \sum_{k=0}^{n} |\lambda|^k \| R \|^k \frac{1}{k!} + \| F \| \sum_{k=0}^{n} |\lambda|^k \| R \|^k ,$$

because $\Sigma_{j=2}^{k} 1/j! \leqslant \Sigma_{j=2}^{\infty} 1/j! = e-2<1$. We therefore conclude that the series (11.11) is convengent for $|\lambda| < 1/\| R \|$.
Let $z \in Z_D$ and $|\lambda| < 1/\| R \|$ be arbitrarily fixed. Formula (11.6) implies that the series

$$\sum_{n=0}^{\infty} \lambda^n R^n z = z \sum_{n=0}^{\infty} \lambda^n R^n e \tag{11.13}$$

is convergent. Denote by $e_\lambda(z)$ its sum. Since $R^n z \in Z_D$ for all

$n \in \{0\} \cup \mathbb{N}$ and $De_\lambda(z) = D\,\Sigma_{n=0}^{\infty} \lambda^n R^n z = \Sigma_{n=0}^{\infty} \lambda^n DR^n z =$
$\Sigma_{n=1}^{\infty} \lambda^n R^{n-1} z = \lambda\,\Sigma_{k=0}^{\infty} \lambda^k R^k z = \lambda e_\lambda(z)$;

$$Fe_\lambda(z) = F \sum_{n=0}^{\infty} \lambda^n R^n z = \sum_{n=0}^{\infty} \lambda^n FR^n z = Fz = z.$$

We conclude that $e_\lambda(z)$ are exponential elements for D. Suppose now that F is multiplicative. Then Formula (11.10) implies that for all $\lambda \in \mathbb{C}$

$$\left\| \sum_{n=0}^{\infty} \lambda^n R^n e \right\| = \left\| \sum_{n=0}^{\infty} \lambda^n \frac{(Re)^n}{n!} \right\| \leqslant \sum_{n=0}^{\infty} |\lambda|^n \frac{\|R\|^n}{n!} = e^{|\lambda|\,\|R\|} .$$

Then the series (11.11) is convergent for all $\lambda \in \mathbb{C}$ and exponential elements exist also for all $\lambda \in \mathbb{C}$ and are of the form (11.12).

<u>Example 11.1.</u> Suppose that $X = C[0,T]$, $T > 0$, $D = d/dt$, $(Fx)(t) = (1/T)\int_0^T x(s)ds$ for $x \in X$. The corresponding right inverse is of the form: $(Rx)(t) = \int_o^t x(s)ds + (1/T)\int_0^T (T-s)x(s)ds$ for $x \in X$. The operator F is not multiplicative, however it satisfies Condition (11.4). It is easy to verify that $R \notin V(X)$. Indeed, if $x(t) = e^{2\pi ikt/T}$ then $(I-2\pi ikR/T)x = 0$ for all integers k. Since $\|R\| = (3/2)T$, we conclude that for $|\lambda| < 2/3T$ exponential elements exist.

<u>Corollary 11.2.</u> Suppose that all assumptions of Corollary 11.2 are satisfied. Then R-shifts exist and are of the form

$$S_h R^k z = \frac{z}{k!}(Re-he)^k \quad \text{for all } z \in Z_D,\ k \in \{0\} \cup \mathbb{N}, \qquad (11.14)$$

$h \in A(\mathbb{R})$.

Indeed, by the definition of R-shifts Property 4.6 and Corollary 11.2 we have:

$$S_h R^k e = \sum_{j=0}^{k} \frac{(-1)^{k-j}}{(k-j)!} h^{k-j} R^j e = \sum_{j=0}^{k} \frac{(-1)^{k-j}}{(k-j)!} h^{k-j} \frac{(Re)^j}{j!}$$

$$= \frac{1}{k!} \sum_{j=0}^{k} k! \frac{(-1)^{k-j}}{(k-j)!j!} h^{k-j} (Re)^j = \frac{1}{k!} \sum_{j=0}^{k} \binom{k}{j} (-h)^{k-j} (Re)^j$$

$$= \frac{1}{k!} (Re-he)^k .$$

<u>Corollary 11.3.</u> Suppose that all assumptions of Theorem 11.2 are satisfied and the operator F is multiplicative. Then D-shifts exist and coincide with R-shifts. In particular, we have

$$S_h e_\lambda(z) = z\, e^{\lambda(Re-he)} \quad \text{where } e^{\lambda(Re-he)} = \sum_{n=0}^{\infty} \lambda^n \frac{(Re-he)^n}{n!}$$

$$\text{for all } \lambda \in \mathbb{C},\ z \in Z_D. \qquad (11.15)$$

The proof is an immediate consequence of Point 2° of Theorem 11.2, Corollary 11.2 and Formulae (11.13). Indeed, for all $\lambda \in C$, $z \in Z_D$ we have

$$S_h \sum_{n=0}^{\infty} \lambda^n R^n e = \sum_{n=0}^{\infty} \lambda^n S_n R^n e = \sum_{n=0}^{\infty} \lambda^n \frac{(Re-he)^n}{n!} =$$

$$= e^{\lambda(Re-he)} ,$$

which implies

$$S_h e_\lambda(x) = S_h\left(z \sum_{n=0}^{\infty} \lambda^n R^n e\right) = ze^{\lambda(Re-he)} .$$

In a similar way, as in Corollary 11.2 we obtain

Corollary 11.4. Suppose that all assumptions of Theorem 11.1 are satisfied. Then R-shifts exist and are of the form

$$S_h R^k z =$$

$$\frac{z}{k!}(Re-he)^k - z \sum_{j=0}^{k} \frac{(-1)^{k-j}}{(k-j)!} h^{k-j} \sum_{m=2}^{j} \frac{1}{m!} R^{j-m} F[(Re)^m] \tag{11.16}$$

for all $z \in Z_D$, $k \in \{0\} \cup \mathbb{N}$, $h \in A(\mathbb{R})$.

We shall consider now Dh_o-rings.

Theorem 11.3. Suppose that $D \in R(X)$, where X is a Dh_o-ring with unit e and F is an initial operator for D corresponding to an $R \in \mathscr{R}_D$. Then

1° The formula for integration by parts is of the form

$$R(xDy) = xy - F(xy) \quad \text{for } x,y \in \mathscr{D}_D . \tag{11.17}$$

2° If F satisfies Condition (11.4) then

$$R^n z = zR^n e \quad \text{for all } z \in Z_D,\ n \in \mathbb{N} \tag{11.18}$$

and

$$R^n e = (Re)^n - \sum_{k=2}^{n} R^{n-k} F[(Re)^k] \quad \text{for all } n \geq 2 . \tag{11.19}$$

3° If F is multiplicative then Formula (11.8) holds and

$$R^n e = (Re)^n . \tag{11.20}$$

Proof: Since $D(xy) = xDy$ for all $x,y \in \mathscr{D}_D$, we have

$$xy - F(xy) = (I-F)(xy) = RD(xy) = R(xDy),$$

which implies Formula (1.17). If in (1.17) we put $x = z \in \ker D$, $y = Re$ we find $Dy = e$ and $Rz = zRe - F(zRe)$. Suppose now that Condition (11.4) is satisfied. Then $Rz = zRe - zFRe = zRe$, which proves Formula (11.18) for $n = 1$. Suppose that this Formula is true for an arbitrarily fixed positive integer n. Then $R^{n+1}z = R(R^n z) = R(zR^n e) = zR(R^n e) = zR^{n+1}e$ which implies that $R^n z = zR^n e$ for all $n \in \mathbb{N}$. In order to prove Formula (11.19) observe that $R^2 e = R(Re) = R(eRe) = (Re)(Re) - F[(Re)(Re)] = (Re)^2 - F[(Re)^2]$, because $e = D(Re)$. Suppose now formula (11.12) to be true for an arbitrarily fixed $n \geq 2$. Then

$$R^{n+1}e = R[(Re)^n] - R \sum_{k=2}^{n} R^{n-k} F[(Re)^k] =$$

$$= R[e(Re)^n] - \sum_{k=2}^{n} R^{n+1-k} F[(Re)^k] =$$

$$= (Re)^{n+1} - F[(Re)^{n+1} - \sum_{k=2}^{n} R^{n+1-k} F[(Re)^k] =$$

$$= (Re)^{n+1} - \sum_{k=2}^{n+1} R^{n+1-k} F[(Re)^k],$$

which was to be proved. If the operator F is multiplicative, we obtain in the same way as in the proof of Corollary 11.1 that $F[(Re)^k] = 0$ for all $k \in \mathbb{N}$, which implies Formula (11.20).

Corollary 11.5. If all assumptions of Theorem 11.3 are satisfied and F satisfies Condition (11.4) then R-shifts exist and are of the form

$$S_h R^k z = z \sum_{j=0}^{k} \frac{(-1)^{k-j}}{(k-j)!} h^{k-j} \{(Re)^j - \sum_{m=2}^{j} R^{j-m} R[(Re)^m]\} \tag{11.21}$$

$$\text{for all } z \in \ker D,\ k \in \{0\} \cup \mathbb{N},\ h \in A(\mathbb{R}) .$$

Corollary 11.6. If all assumptions of Theorem 11.3 are satisfied, and F is multiplicative, then R-shifts exist and are of the form

$$S_h R^j z = z \sum_{j=0}^{k} \frac{(-1)^{k-j}}{(k-j)!} h^{k-j} (Re)^j \quad \text{for all } z \in \ker D, \tag{11.22}$$

$$k \in \{0\} \cup \mathbb{N},\ h \in A(\mathbb{R}).$$

Corollary 11.7. Suppose that all assumptions of Theorem 11.3 are satisfied. Suppose, moreover, that $\mathscr{F} = \mathbb{C}$, X is a Banach algebra (with respect to the structure operations under consideration), the operators F and R are bounded and F either satisfies Condition (11.4) or is multiplicative. Then

1° the series $\Sigma_{n=0}^{\infty} \lambda^n R^n e$ is convergent for all $|\lambda| < 1/\|R\|$

2° exponential elements exist for $|\lambda| < 1/\|R\|$ and are of the form:

$$e_\lambda(z) = z \sum_{n=0}^{\infty} \lambda^n R^n e \text{ , where } z \in \ker D,\ \lambda \in \mathbb{C}; \tag{11.23}$$

3° $R \notin V(X)$ (even in the case when F is multiplicative);

4° D-shifts exist for $|\lambda| < 1/\|R\|$

Proofs of Corollaries 11.5, 11.6, 11.7 proceed on similar lines to those for Leibniz rings.

Consider now QL-rings with unit e. We have by our assumption

$$De = D(e^2) = eDe + eDe + d(De)(De) = 2De + d(De)^2,$$

which implies

$$(De)(e + dDe) = 0 \ , \quad d \neq 0 \ . \tag{11.24}$$

(cf. Dudek [1]. He has also shown that the case when $De \neq 0$ and $e + dDe \neq 0$ can be reduced in the large class of QL-rings to cases when either $De = 0$ or $e + dDe = 0$).

We now examine the case when $e + dDe = 0$, since this equality yields very simple results.

Theorem 11.4. Suppose that $D \in R(X)$, where X is a QL-ring with unit e satisfying the condition

$$e + dDe = 0 \; , \quad d \neq 0 \; , \tag{11.25}$$

and F is an initial operator for D corresponding to an $R \in \mathscr{R}_D$. Then

1° $Fe \in Z_D$;

2° If the operator $I + dR$ is invertible then e is an exponential element for D corresponding to the eigenvalue -d, i.e.

$$e_{-d}(z) = (I+dR)^{-1}z = e, \text{ where } z = Fe;$$

3° If $R \in V(X)$ then either $d = 1$ or $d = -1$;

4° The following Formula holds:

$$R^n e = \frac{(-1)^n}{d^n}\left(e + \sum_{k=0}^{n-1} (-1)^{k+1} d^k R^k Fe\right) \quad \text{for all} \quad n \in \mathbb{N}. \tag{11.26}$$

Proof: Equality (11.25) implies that $0 = (1/d)D(dRe + e) = (1/d)D(I+dR)e$. Thus $(I+dR)e = z$, where $z \in Z_D$. Acting on both sides of this equality with the operator F we find: $z = Fz = Fe + dFRe = Fe$. If the operator $I+dR$ is invertible then we have: $e = (I+dR)^{-1}z = (I+dR)^{-1}Fe = e_{-d}(Fe)$. Suppose now that $R \in V(X)$. Then for all $z_1, z_2 \in Z_D$, $\lambda, \mu \in$ there exists $z_3 \in Z_D$ such that

$$e_\lambda(z_1)e_\mu(z_2) = e_{\lambda+\mu+d\lambda\mu}(z_3)$$

(cf. the author [10]). This implies that there exists a $z \in Z_D$ such that

$$e_{-d}(Fe) = e = e^2 = e_{-d}(Fe)e_{-d}(Fe) = e_{-d-d+d(-d)^2}(z) =$$

$$= e_{-2d+d^3}(z) ,$$

and we have the equality $e_{-d}(Fe) = e_{-2d+d^3}(z)$ which can be rewritten as follows:

$$[I + (2d-d^3)R]Fe = (I + dR)z .$$

Operating on both sides of this equality with the operator F we obtain $z = Fe$ and $e_{-d}(Fe) = e_{-2d+d^3}(Fe)$. We therefore conclude that $-d = -2d+d^3$, i.e. $d^3-d = 0$. But $d \neq 0$, and hence $d^2-1 = 0$ and so we obtain either $d = 1$ or $d = -1$.
The equality $(I+dR)e = Fe$ implies that $Re = -(1/d)(I-F)e = (-1/d)(e-Fe)$. This proves Formula (11.26) for $n = 1$. In order to prove that this formula is true for all $n \in \mathbb{N}$ write:
$\hat{e} = (dRf-F+I)e$. Observe that $R\hat{e} = R(dRF-F+I)e = dR^2Fe - RFe + Re$ $= dR^2Fe - RFe + (1/d)(Fe-e) = dR^2Fe - (1/d)(dRe-Fe+e) = dR^2Fe - (1/d)\hat{e}$.
Suppose now Formula (11.26) to be true for an arbitrarily fixed $n \geq 1$. Then

$$R^{n+1}e = \frac{(-1)^n}{d^n}(Re + \sum_{k=0}^{n-1} (-1)^{k+1} d^k R^{k+1} Fe) =$$

$$= \frac{(-1)^n}{d^n}(R\hat{e} + \sum_{k=2}^{n-1} (-1)^{k+1} d^k R^{k+1} Fe) =$$

$$= \frac{(-1)^n}{d^n}(dR^2Fe - \frac{1}{d}\hat{e} + \sum_{k=2}^{n-1} (-1)^{k+1} d^k R^{k+1} Fe) =$$

$$= \frac{(-1)^{n+1}}{d^{n+1}} (\hat{e} - d^2R^2Fe + \sum_{k=2}^{n-1} (-1)^{k+2} d^{k+1} R^{k+1} Fe) =$$

$$= \frac{(-1)^{n+1}}{d^{n+1}} (\hat{e} - d^2R^2Fe + \sum_{j=3}^{n} (-1)^{j+1} d^j R^j Fe) =$$

$$= \frac{(-1)^{n+1}}{d^{n+1}} (e + \sum_{j=0}^{n} (-1)^{j+1} d^j R^j Fe) ,$$

which was to be proved.

Corollary 11.8. Suppose that all assumptions of Theorem 1.4 are satisfied and that F satisfies Condition (11.4). Then

1° For all $z \in Z_D$, $n \in \mathbb{N}$ we have

$$R^n z = zR^n e, \tag{11.27}$$

2° R-shifts exist and are of the form:

$$S_h R^k z = (-1)^k z [\frac{h^k}{k!} e + \sum_{j=1}^{k} \frac{h^{k-j}}{(k-j)! d^j} (e + \sum_{m=0}^{j-1} (-1)^{m+1} d^m R^m Fe)] \tag{11.28}$$

for all $h \in A(\mathbb{R})$, $z \in Z_D$, $k \in \{0\} \cup \mathbb{N}$.

Proof: Since by our assumptions Conditions (11.1) and (11.4) are satisfied then we have for all $x,y \in \mathscr{D}_D$

$$xy - F(xy) = (I-F)(xy) = RD(xy) = R(xDy) + R(yDx) + dR[(Dx)(Dy)]$$

and for $x = z \in \ker D$, $y = Re$ (since $Dx = 0$, $Dy = e$, $RF = 0$),

$$zRe = zRe - zFRe = zRe - F(zRe) = R(zDRe) + R[(Re)(Dz) + dR(eDz)]$$

$$= Rz \ .$$

Suppose Formula (11.27) to be true for an arbitrarily fixed positive integer n. Then $R^{n+1}z = R^n(Rz) = R^n(zRe) = zR^n(Re) =$ $= zR^{n+1}e$. We therefore conclude that $R^n z = zR^n e$ for arbitrary $n \in \mathbb{N}$ and $z \in Z_D$. Formulae (11.26) and (11.27) together imply that for all $h \in A(\mathbb{R})$, $k \in \{0\} \cup \mathbb{N}$ and $z \in Z_D$ we have

$$S_h R^k z = \sum_{j=0}^{k} \frac{(-1)^{k-j}}{(k-j)!} h^{k-j} R^j z = z \sum_{j=0}^{k} \frac{(-1)^{k-j}}{(k-j)!} h^{k-j} R^j e =$$

$$= z \frac{(-1)^k}{k!} h^k e + z \sum_{j=1}^{k} \frac{(-1)^{k-j}}{(k-j)!} h^{k-j} \frac{(-1)^j}{d^j} (e + \sum_{m=0}^{j-1} (-1)^{m+1} d^m R^m Fe)$$

$$= (-1)^k z [\frac{h^k}{k!} e + \sum_{j=1}^{k} \frac{h^{k-j}}{(k-j)!d^j} (e + \sum_{m=0}^{j-1} (-1)^{m+1} d^m R^m Fe)] \ .$$

In a similar way, as before, we prove

Corollary 11.9. Suppose that all assumptions of Theorem 11.4 are satisfied and the operator F satisfies Condition (11.4). Suppose, moreover, that $\mathcal{F} = \mathbb{C}$, X is a Banach algebra (with respect to the structure operations under consideration) and the operators F and R are bounded and $\| e \| = 1$. Then for all $|\lambda| < d/\| R \|$ the series $\Sigma_{n=0}^{\infty} \lambda^n R^n e$ is convergent, exponential elements exist and are of the form: $e_\lambda(z) = z \Sigma_{n=0}^{\infty} \lambda^n R^n e$, where $z \in Z_D$, and D-shifts exist.

QL-rings with the property De = 0 are much more difficult to examine and the following is an open question: Find a recursive formula for $R^n e$ ($n \in \mathbb{N}$). Without such a formula we cannot say anything more about shifts.

We have proved* the following theorem: 1) If X is a commutative linear ring with unit e, $D \in R(X)$ and satisfies the Leibniz condition (i.e. X is an L-ring) and $R \in \mathscr{R}_D \cap V(X)$ then there exists an operator $T \in L_0(X)$ such that DT-TD = I, namely Tx = xRe for all $x \in \mathscr{D}_D$. The assumption that $R \in V(X)$ is not necessary. Indeed, if $R \in \mathscr{R}_D$ is arbitrarily fixed then for all $x \in \mathscr{D}_D$ we have: DTx - TDx = D(xRe) - (Re)Dx = (Dx)(Re)+xDRe - (Re)(Dx) = x·e = x. The arbitrariness of x implies DT-TD = I. Having already proved this property we can show, in the same way as in the mentioned paper, that if X is a complete linear metric space, $D \in R(X)$ and X is an L-ring (with respect to the same addition operation) then D is not continuous. Moreover, if X ≠ ker D then X ≠ ker P(D) for every polynomial P(t) with coefficients in the scalar field $\mathscr{F}$ under consideration such that P(0) = 0, P(t) ≠ at for all t (provided that the field $\mathscr{F}$ is algebraically closed). The existence of the operator T could be useful in order to find an explicit formula for R-shifts, since

---

* cf. the author, Algebraic derivative and abstract differential equations. Anais da Academia Brasileiva de Ciencias, 42 (1970), 403-409; Theorem 3.4.

we have

$$T^n z = z(Re)^n \quad \text{for all } z \in Z_D,\ n \in \mathbb{N}. \qquad (11.29)$$

Indeed, $Tz = zRe$, by our definition. Suppose Formula (11.29) to be true for an arbitrary positive integer n. Then $T^{n+1}z = T(T^n z) = (Re)z(Re)^n = z(Re)^{n+1}$.

12 Remarks on controllability and observability of systems with shifts

Suppose that X and U are linear spaces over the same field of scalars. Denote by $L_0(U,X)$ the set of linear operators defined on U and with range in X. Let $D \in R(X)$, let F be an initial operator for D corresponding to an $R \in \mathscr{R}_D$ and let $A \in L_0(X)$, $B \in L_0(u)$. Here and in the sequel we shall assume that the operator I-RA is *invertible*. Consider the system

$$Dx = Ax + Bu, \quad Fx = x_0, \quad x_0 \in Z_D \ . \tag{12.1}$$

By our assumption, the system (12.1) has a unique solution $x = \Phi(x_0,u)$ for arbitrarily fixed $u \in U$, $x_0 \in Z_D$, where

$$\Phi(x_0,u) = (I-RA)^{-1}(x_0+RBu), \quad x_0 \in Z_D, \quad u \in U. \tag{12.2}$$

X and U will be called the *state* and *control* space, respectively, and $x \in X$, $u \in U$, $x_0 \in Z_D$ the *state* or *output*, *control* or *input* and the *initial state*, respectively.

We shall give here some definitions and theorems (without proofs) due to Nguyên Dinh Quyêt (cf. [1], [2], [4]).

A *transfer operator* for the system (12.1) is a matrix operator defined as follows:

$$G = [(I-RA)^{-1}, \ (I-RA)^{-1}RB] \ .$$

It can be proved that transfer operators have similar properties to those of transfer functions for systems described by ordinary differential operators.

A state $x \in X$ is said to be *attainable* from an initial state $x_o \in Z_D$ if there exists a control $u \in U$ such that $x = \Phi(x_o, u)$. The set $\Phi(x_o, U) = \{\Phi(x_o, u) : u \in U\}$ is called the *attainability set* from the initial state x_o.

Let X' be the space of all linear (i.e. additive and homogeneous) functionals defined on the space X. We say that X^+ is a *conjugate* to X if X^+ is an arbitrary *total* subspace of X', i.e. if the condition $\xi(x) = 0$ for all $\xi \in X^+$ implies $x = 0$ (for $x \in X$). An operator $T^+ \in L_o(X^+)$ is said to be conjugate to an operator $T \in L_o(X)$ if it satisfies the following condition:

$$(T^+\xi)(X) = \xi(Tx) \quad \text{for all } x \in X,\ \xi \in X^+ . \tag{12.3}$$

Here and in the sequel we assume that conjugate operators preserve the conjugate space, i.e. $T^+X^+ \subset X^+$ (cf. the author and S. Rolewicz [3]). For instance, if X is a Banach space then the set X^* of linear and bounded functionals defined on X is a conjugate space for X. The space X' itself is a conjugate space for X by our definition.

Proposition 12.1. Every state $x \in X$ is attainable from a given initial state $x_o \in Z_D$ if and only if $\ker B^+R^+[(I-RA)^{-1}]^+ = \{0\}$.

Suppose that $F_1 \in \mathcal{F}_D$ and $F_1 \neq F$. We say that the system (12.1) is *F_1-controllable* if for every initial state $x_o \in Z_D$ we have $\{F_1\Phi(x_o, u) : u \in U\} = Z_D$. In other words, the system (12.1) is F_1-controllable if from every initial state x_o we can reach an arbitrary *final* state x_1 by means of the initial operator F_1, i.e. if $x_1 = F_1(x_o,u)$ for a $u \in U$.

Theorem 12.1. If $\ker B^+R^+[(I-RA)^{-1}]^+ \overline{F}_1^+ = \{0\}$, where $\overline{F}_1^+$ denotes the restriction of F_1 to the set $U_1 = (I-RA)^{-1}RBU$, then the system (12.1) is F_1-controllable.

If $\dim X, \dim U < +\infty$ then the condition $\ker B^+R^+[(I-RA)^{-1}]^+\overline{F}_1^+ = \{0\}$ is just the well-known Kalman rank condition.

The system (12.1) is said to be *stationary* if A and B are stationary (cf. Section 10).

Corollary 12.1. If the system (12.1) is stationary and if $\ker B^+[(I-RA)]^{-1}\overline{F}_1^+ = \{0\}$, then this system is F_1-controllable.

Theorem 12.2. If the system (12.1) is F_1-controllable then it is F_2-controllable for all $F_2 \in \mathscr{F}_D^o$, where

$$\mathscr{F}_D^o = \{\tilde{F} \in \mathscr{F}_D : \forall_{z \in Z_D} \exists_{y \in X} F_2\tilde{R}y = z,\ \tilde{R} \in \mathscr{R}_D,\ \tilde{F}\tilde{R} = 0\}.$$

Now consider the system (12.1) together with an output $y = Hx$, $H \in L_o(X)$, i.e. the system

$$Dx = Ax + Bu,\quad Fx = x_o \in Z_D,\quad y = Hx, \tag{12.4}$$

where $A, H \in L_o(X)$, $B \in L_o(U,X)$, $D \in R(X)$ and F is an initial operator for D corresponding to an $R \in \mathscr{R}_D$ such that the operator $I-AR$ is invertible. To every solution $x = \Phi(x_o,u)$ of the system (12.1) there corresponds an output of the form

$y = H\Phi(x_o,u) = H(I-RA)^{-1}(x_o+RBu)$. The system (12.4) is said to be *observable* if for a given input u and output y there exists a unique initial state $x_o \in Z_D$ such that $y = H\Phi(x_o,u)$.

Theorem 12.3. The system (12.4) is observable if and only if $\ker H(I-RA)^{-1} = \{0\}$.

If the system (12.1) is stationary then we can determine a system dual to the system (12.4) in order to prove that the system (12.4) is observable if and only if the dual system is F_1-controllable.

Suppose now that X and U are Banach spaces and the operators $(I-RA)^{-1}$, RB and H are bounded. For an arbitrary set $S \subset X$ and $\varepsilon > 0$ we denote by $N_\varepsilon(S)$ the ε-neighbourhood of S, i.e. the set $N_\varepsilon(S) = \{x \in X : \|x-s\| < \varepsilon \text{ for all } s \in S\}$. Suppose that $F_1 \neq F$ is an initial operator for D. Then the system (12.4) is stable if for every $\varepsilon > 0$ there exists a $\delta > 0$ and an $S \subset Z_D$ such that $F_1\Phi(x_o,U) \subset N_\varepsilon(S)$ for all $x_o \in Z_D$. The system (12.4) is F_1-output-stable if for every $\varepsilon > 0$ there exists a $\delta > 0$ and $S \subset Z_D$ such that $HF_1\Phi(x_o,U) \subset N_\varepsilon(HS)$ for all $x_o \in Z_D$.

Theorem 12.4. If the system (12.4) is F_1-stable then it is F_1-output-stable. If the system (12.4) is observable and F_1-output-stable then it is F_1-stable.

Nguyễn Dinh Quyêt also gave necessary and sufficient conditions for the existence of an optimal control for a quadratic performance functional subject to constraints of the form (12.1) in Hilbert spaces (cf. [4]).

We have considered systems (12.1) and (12.4) which are of

very simple form. However, this is sufficient since a superposition of right invertible operators and polynomials in right invertible operators with operator coefficients satisfying conditions of Corollary 0.3 are again right invertible operators (cf. also Theorem 0.5). We therefore can reduce more complicated problems to these of the form (12.1) and (12.4).

We shall consider now periodic systems with shifts.

<u>Theorem 12.5.</u> Suppose that X is a linear space (over $\mathbb{C}$), U is a linear subspace of X,* $D \in R(X)$, F is an initial operator of D corresponding to an $R \in \mathscr{R}_D$, $\{S_h\}_{h \in A(\mathbb{R})} \subset L_o(X)$ is a family of D-invariant R-shifts, the operators $A_o, A_1, \ldots, A_{N-1} \in L_o(X)$ and $B_o, B_1, \ldots, B_{N-1} \in L_o(U,X)$ are S_h-periodic for an $h \in A(\mathbb{R})$, i.e. we have

$$A_j S_h = S_h A_j, \quad B_j S_h = S_h B_j \quad (j = 0,1,\ldots,N-1) .$$

Write:

$$X_h = \{x \in X : S_h^N x = x\}; \; X_h^1 = X_h \cap \mathscr{D}_D; \; U_h = X_h \cap U , \quad (12.5)$$

$$A(S_h) = \sum_{j=0}^{N-1} A_j S_h^j = \sum_{j=0}^{N-1} A_j S_{h_j}; \; B(S_h) = \sum_{j=0}^{N-1} B_j S_h^j = \sum_{j=0}^{N-1} B_j S_h , \quad (12.6)$$

---

*The assumption that U is a linear subspace of X is not very restrictive for our considerations, because in the general case we can consider a linear space Y containing both X and U and the corresponding extensions of the operators under consideration.

(cf. Formula (3.6)). Consider the periodic system

$$Dx = A(S_h)x + B(S_h)u \ , \ Fx = x_o, \ x_o \in Z_D \ . \tag{12.7}$$

Then in the space X_h the system (12.7) is equivalent to N independent systems

$$Dx_j = A(\varepsilon^j)x_j + B(\varepsilon^j)u_j \ , \ Fx_j = \delta_{jN} \ x_o \ (j = 1,2,\dots,N) \tag{12.8}$$

considered in spaces X_j, U_j, respectively, where

$$x_j = P_j x, \ u_j = P_j u, \ \delta_{jN} = \begin{cases} 0 \text{ for } j \neq N \\ 1 \text{ for } j = N \end{cases}, \ X_j = P_j X_h \ , \ U_j = P_j U_h \tag{12.9}$$

$\varepsilon = e^{2\pi i/N}$, and the projectors $P_1,\dots,P_N$ are determined by the decomposition (2.4), i.e.

$$P_j = \frac{1}{N} \sum_{k=0}^{N-1} \varepsilon^{kj} S_k^j = \frac{1}{N} \sum_{k=0}^{N-1} \varepsilon^{-kj} S_{hj} \quad (j = 1,2,\dots,N). \tag{12.10}$$

Proof: Observe that for all $z \in Z_D$ we have $S_h z = z$ (cf. Theorem 3.1). Then

$$P_j x_o = \frac{1}{N} \sum_{k=0}^{N-1} \varepsilon^{-kj} S_h^j x_o = \frac{1}{N} \sum_{k=0}^{N-1} \varepsilon^{-kj} \ S_{hj} x_o = \left(\frac{1}{N} \sum_{k=0}^{N-1} \varepsilon^{-kj}\right) x_0 =$$

$$= \begin{cases} \dfrac{1}{N} \dfrac{(\varepsilon^j)^N - 1}{\varepsilon - 1} x_o = 0 & \text{for } j \neq N \ , \\[2ex] \dfrac{1}{N} N \ x_o = x_o & \text{for } j = N \ , \end{cases}$$

because $\varepsilon^N = 1$. The remainder of the proof follows along the same lines as the proof of Corollary 2.3.

Corollary 12.2. Suppose that all assumptions of Theorem 12.5 are satisfied. Write:

$$R_N = (I + FS_{Nh} + \frac{1}{Nh} RFS_{Nh})R \ , \ D_N = D - \frac{1}{Nh} FS_{Nh} \ , \qquad (12.11)$$

(cf. Formula 3.20). If each of the operators $I-R_N A(\varepsilon^j)$ is invertible in the space X_j $(j = 1,2,\dots,N)$ then for every $u \in U_j$, every one of Equations (12.8) has a unique solution of the form

$$x_j = [I-R_N A(\varepsilon^j)]^{-1}[R_N B(\varepsilon^j)u_j - \frac{1}{Nh} \delta_{jN} x_o] \ (j = 1,2,\dots,N) \qquad (12.12)$$

belonging to the space X_j. Moreover, the system (12.7) has a unique S^N-periodic solution for every $u \in U_h$ which is of the form

$$x = \sum_{j=1}^{N} x_j = \sum_{j=1}^{N} [I-R_N A(\varepsilon^j)]^{-1}[R_N B(\varepsilon^j)P_j u - \frac{1}{Nh} x_o], \qquad (12.13)$$

(where x_j, u_j, ε are defined in Theorem 12.5).

Proof: By our assumptions and Theorem 12.5 the system (12.7) is equivalent to the N systems (12.8). Let $1 \leqslant j \leqslant N$ be arbitrarily fixed. Consider the j-th system (12.8) in the space $X_j \subset X_h$. Since $S_{Nh} x_j = S_h^N x_j = x_j$ and $D_N x_j = Dx_j - (1/Nh) FS_{Nh} x_j =$ $= Dx_j - (1/Nh) Fx_j = A(\varepsilon^j)x_j + B(\varepsilon^j)u_j - (1/Nh) Fx_j$, Theorem 3.4

implies that $x_j = R_N D_N x_j = R_N[A(\varepsilon^j)x_j + B(\varepsilon^j)u_j - (1/Nh)\delta_{jN}\, x_o]$.

The operators $A(\varepsilon^j)$ and $B(\varepsilon^j)$ preserve the space X_j, the operator R_N preserves the space X_h. Therefore, if we assume that the operator $I-R_N A(\varepsilon^j)$ is invertible in the space X_j, i.e. that its inverse belongs to $L_o(X_j)$, we conclude that the j-th system (12.8) has a unique solution in the space X_j, for every $u_j \in U_j$, which is of the form (12.11). This implies that the system (12.7) has a unique S^N-periodic solution for every $u \in U_h$ which is of the form

$$x = \sum_{j=1}^{N} x_j = \sum_{j=1}^{N} [I-R_N A(\varepsilon^j)]^{-1}[R_N B(\varepsilon^j)u_j - \frac{1}{Nh}\delta_{jN} x_o] =$$

$$= \sum_{j=1}^{N} [I-R_N A(\varepsilon^j)]^{-1}[R_N B(\varepsilon^j)P_j u - \frac{1}{Nh} x_o] .$$

<u>Corollary 12.3.</u> Suppose that all assumptions of Theorem 12.5 are satisfied and that $A_o = A_1 = \ldots = A_{N-1} = 0$. Then the system (12.7) has a unique S^N-periodic solution for every $u \in U_n$ which is of the form

$$x = R_N B(S_h)u - \frac{1}{Nh} x_o . \qquad (12.14)$$

Indeed, in our case

$$x = \sum_{j=1}^{N} R_N B(\varepsilon^j)P_j u - \frac{1}{Nh} x_o = R_N[\sum_{j=1}^{N} B(\varepsilon^j)P_j]u - \frac{1}{Nh} x_o =$$

$$= R_N B(S_n)u - \frac{1}{Nh} x_o .$$

Corollary 12.3 and Theorem 12.1 together imply the following

Theorem 12.6. Suppose that all assumptions of Theorem 12.5 are satisfied and that operators $I-R_N A(\varepsilon^j)$ are invertible in the space X_j, respectively $(j = 1,2,\ldots,N)$. Let $F_1 \in \mathscr{F}_D$ and $F_1 \neq F$. If

$$\ker B(\varepsilon^j)^+ R_N^+ \{[I-R_N A(\varepsilon^j)]^{-1}\}^+ \overline{F}_j^+ = \{0\} \text{ for } j = 1,2,\ldots,N, \tag{12.15}$$

where $\overline{F}_j^+$ denote the restrictions of F_1 to the sets $[I-R_N A(\varepsilon^j)]^{-1} R_N B(\varepsilon^j)U_j$, then the system (12.7) is F_1-controllable in the space X_h.

Indeed, by our assumption, the j-th system (12.8) is F_1-controllable in the space X_j $(j = 1,2,\ldots,n)$, i.e. we have for a given $x_o \in Z_D$

$$\{F_1 [I-R_N A(\varepsilon^j)]^{-1} [R_N B(\varepsilon^j) u_j - \frac{1}{Nh} x_o] : u_j \in U_j\} = Z_D.$$

Therefore,

$$\{F_1 \sum_{j=1}^{N} [I-R_N A(\varepsilon^j)]^{-1} [R_N B(\varepsilon^j) P_j u - \frac{1}{Nh} x_o] :$$

$$u = \sum_{j=1}^{N} P_j u = \sum_{j=1}^{N} u_j \in U\} = Z_D ,$$

which implies the F_1-controllability of the system (12.7).

Corollary 12.3 and Theorem 12.3 together imply

Theorem 12.7. Suppose that all assumptions of Theorem 12.5 are satisfied and that the operators $I-R_N A(\varepsilon^j)$ are invertible in the space X_j, respectively ($j = 1,2,\dots,N$). Then the system (12.7) with the output

$$y = Hx, \text{ where } H \in L_o(X),\ HS_h = S_h H \tag{12.16}$$

is observable in the space X_h if and only if

$$\ker H[I-R_N A(\varepsilon^j)]^{-1} = \{0\} \quad \text{for } j = 1,2,\dots,N\ . \tag{12.17}$$

Similar results can be obtained in the spaces of exponential-periodic elements and polynomial-exponential-periodic elements if we assume that S_h is not only an R-shift but also a D-shift and we apply the results of Sections 8 and 9. In order to find an optimal periodic, or exponential-periodic control in the case of a quadratic performance functional in a Hilbert space we should apply the results of Nguyên Dinh Quyêt [3] and the method used in the author's book [3]. However, we should point out that this is only a starting point in order to study controllability, observability and other problems connected with systems described by right invertible operators with shifts.

We should mention also that just recently Staniaszek [4] proved necessary and sufficient conditions for the existence of an optimal control in the case of a non-linear functional with non-linear functional with non-linear constraints described by right invertible operators in Banach spaces and that these results can be easily extended for non-linear periodic problems. This extension could be done, for instance, by application of Corollary 8.2 and the method used for non-linear periodic problems in the author's book [3]. The same is true concerning exponential-periodic problems. To finish these remarks we should recall, and point out again, that the word 'periodic' used here has a much more general meaning than the classical one. For instance, any transformation of arguments which is an involution of order n is, in that sense, periodic.

References

M. F. Arscott

1 *Periodic differential equations.* Pergamon Press, Oxford, 1964.

H. Bart

1 Periodic strongly continuous semigroups. Annali di Matematica Pura e Applicata (IV), 65 (1977), 311-318.

H. Bart and S. Golberg

1 Characterization of almost periodic strongly continuous groups and semi-groups. Math. Annalen, 236 (1978), 105-116.

L. Berg

1 Zum Umkehrung "periodischer" Operatoren, ZAMM, 55 (1975), 63-66.

A. Coddington and N. Levinson

1 *Theory of Ordinary Differential Equations.* McGraw-Hill Book Co. New York-Toronto-London, 1955.

P. E. Conner and E. E. Floyd

1 *Differentiable Periodic Maps.* Springer Verlag, Berlin-Göttingen-Heidelbert, 1964.

Z. Dudek

1 Some properties of Wronskian in D-R spaces of the type Q-L.I. Demonstratio Math. 11 (1978) (to appear).

V. Hutson and J. S. Pym

1 General Translations Associated with an Operator. Math. Annalen, 187 (1970), 241-258.

E. L. Ince

1 *Ordinary Differential Equations.* (Longmans, Green 1926), London 1927.

Ch. Kahane

1 On Operators commuting with differentiation. Amer. Math. Monthly, 76 (1969), 171-173.

I. Kaplansky

1 *An introduction to Differential Algebra.* Hermann, 1957.

I. I. Kolodner

1 On exp (tA) with A satisfying a polynomial. J. Math. Anal. Appl. 52 (1975), 514-524.

R. G. Koplatadze, T. A. Chanturija

1 On oscillation properties of differential equations with deviating argument (Russian), Institut of Applied Mathematics, Tbilisi State Univ. Tbilisi, 1977.

M. K. Krasnosielskii

1 *Shift operator along trajectories of differential equations* (Russian), Izd. Nauka, Moscow, 1966.

B. M. Levitan

1 *Theory of generalized shift operators* (Russian), Izd. Nauka, Mascow, 1973.

Z. Moszner

1 Structure de l'automate plein, recluit et inversible, Aequationes Math. 9 (1973), 46-59.

2 The translation equation and its application, Demonstratio Math. 6 (1973), 309-327.

Z. Moszner, J. Tabor

1 L'équation de translation sur la structure avec zéro. Annales Polon. Math. 31 (1976), 255-264.

W. Magnus and S. Winter

1 *Hill's Equation*. Interscience, New York, 1966.

E. Muhamadiev

1 On the theory of periodic completely continuous vector fields (Russian). Uspehi Mat. Nauk, 22 (1967), 127-128.

B. Mazbic-Kulma

1 On an equation with reflection of order n. Studia Math. 35 (1970), 69-75.

2 Differential equations in a linear ring. Ibidem. 39 (1971), 157-161.

Nguyên đinh Quyêt

1 On linear systems described by right invertible operators acting in a linear space. Control and Cybernetics, 7, 2 (1978), 33-45.

2 Controllability and observability of linear systems described by the right invertible operators in linear spaces. Ph. dissertation. Preprint No. 113, Institute of Mathematics, Polish Academy of Sciences, October, 1977.

3 A minimizing problem of a quadratic functional for a system described by right invertible operators in Hilbert space. Control and Cybernetics, 7, 3 (1978), 27-36.

4 On the stability and the observability of (D-R)-systems in Banach spaces. Demonstratio Math. 12 (1978) (to appear).

S. D. Poisson

1 Mémoires sur les équations aux differences mélées. Journal de l'École Polytechnique, 6, Cahier 13 (1806), 126-147.

D. Przeworska-Rolewicz

1 Équations avec opérations algébriques. Studia Math. 22 (1963), 337-367.

2 Algebraic derivative and abstract differential equations. Anais Acad. Brasil Ciênc. 42 (1970), 403-409.

3 *Equations with transformed argument. An algebraic approach.* Elsevier Scientific Publish. Co. and PWN-Polish Scientific Publishers, Amsterdam-Warszawa, 1973.

4 Algebraic theory of right invertible operators. Studia Math. 48 (1973), 129-143.

5 Right invertible operators and functional - differential equations with involutions. Demonstratio Math. 5 (1973), 165-177.

6 On linear differential equations with transformed argument solvable by means of right invertible operators. Annales Polonici Math. 29 (1974), 141-148.

7 Extension of Operational Calculus. Control and Cybernetics, 2 (1973), 5-14.

8 Admissible initial operators for superpositions of right invertible operators. Annales Polonici Math. 33 (1976), 113-120.

9 Concerning non-linear equations with right invertible operators. Demonstration Math. 3 (1975), 313-321.

10 On trignometric identity for right invertible operators.

Commentationes Math. 21 (1978), 267-268.

11 *Przestrzenie liniowe i operatory liniowe* (Polish, *Linear spaces and linear operators*), WNT, Warszawa, 1977,

12 *Wstep do Analizy Algebraicznej i jej zastosowań* (Polish, *Introduction to Algebraic Analysis* and its applications), WNT (to appear)

13 D-shift and Generalized Periodic Solutions of Equations with right invertible operators. I. Preprint No. 111. Institute of Mathematics, Polish Academy of Sciences, September 1977, Proceedings of the Conference on Methods of Mathematical Programming, September 1977, (to appear).
II. Preprint No. 122, Institute of Mathematics, Polish Academy of Sciences, December, 1977.
III. Preprint No. 132, Institute of Mathematics, Polish Academy of Sciences, February 1978.

14 Shifts and Periodicity for Right Invertible Operators, Preprint No. 157, Institute of Mathematics, Polish Academy of Sciences, October 1978.

15 Right Inverses and Volterra Operators. Journal of Integral Equations (to appear)

16 Integration of unit in linear rings with right invertible operators. Comptes Rendus. Math. Reports. Royal Soc. of Canada (to appear).

D. Przeworska-Rolewicz and S. Rolewicz

1 On periodic solutions of non-linear differential-difference equations. Bull. Acad. Polon. Sci. 16 (1968), 577-580.

2 On control of linear time lag systems. Studia Math. 32 (1969),

142-152.

3 *Equations in linear spaces*. PWN-Polish Scientific Publishers, Warszawa, 1968.

S. Rolewicz

1 On perturbations of deviations of periodic differential-difference equations in Banach spaces. Studia Math. 47 (1973), 31-35.

S. Staniaszek

1 Optimization in non-linear systems with right invertible operators. Working papers, Institute of Systems Research, Polish Academy of Sciences (to appear).

M. Tasche

1 Abstrakte Differentialgleichungen mit algebraischen Operatoren. Wiss. Zeitschrift. der Universität Rostock, 24 (1975), 1231-1236.

2 Abstrakte lineare Differentialgleichungen mit stationären Operatoren.

3 *Funktionalanalytische Methoden in der Operatorenrechnung*. Nova Acta Leopoldina 49, Halle (Salle), 1978.

H. von Trotha

1 Structure properties of D-R vector spaces. Ph. Dissertation. Preprint No. 102, Institute of Mathematics, Polish Academy of Sciences, Warszawa, November 1977. Dissertationes Math. (to appear).

2 Contractivity in certain D-R spaces. Math. Nachrichten (to appear).

J. Wilkowski

1 On periodic solutions of differential-difference equations with stochastic coefficients. Bull. Acad. Polon. Sci. 21 (1973), 253-256.

A. Włodarska-Dymitruk

1 On a class of solutions of differential-difference equations. Bull. Acad. Polon. Sci. 19 (1971), 29-35.

2 On the control of certain linear almost periodic time lag systems. Ibidem 17 (1971), 587-591.

3 On the control of certain non-linear almost periodic time lag systems. Ibidem 19 (1971), 997-1001.

4 Polynomial - periodic solution of differential-difference equations. Demonstratio Math. 8 (1975), 44-65.

K. Yosida

1 *Functional Analysis*, Springer Verlag, Berlin-Göttingen-Heidlberg 1965.